Biographies

Paul Ham, 37, became Money Editor of The Sunday Times in December 1995, having previously edited two investment magazines published by the Financial Times Group. He has also co-founded several successful financial news letters, including The Money Laundering Bulletin, which traces illegal cash flows, and Governance, aimed at large shareholders.

Nick Gardner, 29, has been a personal finance journalist on The Sunday Times since 1993. In 1995 he was voted Best Young Financial Journalist at the British Golden Pen Awards. In 1996 he was awarded Consumer Journalist of the Year by the British Insurance and Investment Brokers Association (BIIBA).

Giles Pilbrow has drawn cartoons regularly for The Sunday Times for more than six years. He also contributes drawings to Private Eye, The Spectator and other publications. He has produced and written numerous series of Spitting Image and The Big Breakfast, and has published three children's books.

**Also available from
The Sunday Times
on personal finance:**

The Sunday Times Personal Finance Guide to Your Home
by Diana Wright

The Sunday Times Personal Finance Guide to Your Retirement
by Diana Wright

The Sunday Times Personal Finance Guide to Tax-free Savings
by Christopher Gilchrist

THE SUNDAY TIMES

50

ESSENTIAL
QUESTIONS

ON MONEY

1998/1999

Paul Ham & Nick Gardner
Cartoons by Giles Pilbrow

Published by
News International plc
P.O. Box 495,
Virginia Street,
London E1 9XY

Copyright © The Sunday Times 1998
Illustrations Copyright © Giles Pilbrow
The Sunday Times is a registered trademark of Times Newspapers Ltd

No responsibility for loss occasioned to any person acting or refraining
from action as a result of any material in this publication can be accepted
by the editor, author, publisher or The Sunday Times

British Library Cataloguing in Publication Data
A catalogue record for this book is available from the British Library

ISBN 1 902254 09 0

Designed by Dominic James
Cartoons by Giles Pilbrow

Printed and bound in Great Britain by
Clays Ltd, Suffolk

● Contents

● Introduction

Understanding how to make the most of your money and avoid financial disaster is easy. But you would never think so with all the nonsense bandied around by so-called "experts".

The 50 essential questions on money first appeared as a series of articles published in The Sunday Times from May to October 1996. As a result of the very positive response we received to this series we have produced this collection for our readers. The questions and answers included here have been updated to reflect the change in government and the 1998 budget.

In 50 essential questions on money, we demystify finance in a simple Q&A guide. It explains what you need to do, and when, to avoid financial disaster and maximise the return on your savings.

We cover the five foundation blocks of a trouble-free financial life: buying a home, insurance, savings and investment, taxation and retirement planning.

Ten essential questions are devoted to each in five chapters. If you do not know the answers to these questions, you are probably wasting hundreds, if not thousands of pounds because your money is not being invested properly.

For example, you might think pensions are boring and can be put off until the day after tomorrow. But did you know that for every year you put off planning your retirement, you could lose thousands of pounds in retirement income?

By the time you have read this book, you will be well armed to deal with every stage in your life, starting with your children's formative years . . .

FIVE FINANCIAL AGES
Baby

Babies may be cute, but they have a nasty habit of sucking vast amounts of money out of your accounts. You need to consider long term financial planning on their behalf and the cost of education and childcare.

If school fees are your primary concern, you are best advised to invest when they are born, or even before, in a regular savings plan, preferably an aggressively managed personal equity plan (Pep), with-profits endowment fund (see questions 16, 20) or individual savings accounts (ISAs), when they are launched in April 1999.

Peps are more flexible: you can alter, stop and restart your payments, with all income and gains free of tax. Similar flexibility will apply to ISAs. But they can be more vulnerable to stock market movements (see question 14).

With-profits endowment policies offer no payment holidays and impose penalties if you leave the plan early. But they can insulate your savings from stock market falls by "smoothing" the peaks and troughs. This makes them less risky. However, some parents may prefer a safer investment such as National Savings Children's Bonds or even certain Tessa accounts (see question 13).

There are various "packaged" school fee plans on the market, but the packaging itself can be very expensive.

Your children themselves may like their own bank or building society account. Many banks and building societies offer childrens' accounts with the promise of free tokens and gifts. However, these often disguise very low rates of return.

Students and school-leavers

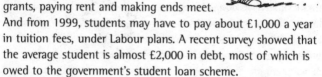

Personal finance is often a low priority for students: life has more pressing concerns than insurance, savings and investments.

But most students will be familiar with the seemingly endless round of loans and grants, paying rent and making ends meet. And from 1999, students may have to pay about £1,000 a year in tuition fees, under Labour plans. A recent survey showed that the average student is almost £2,000 in debt, most of which is owed to the government's student loan scheme.

So students are advised to think carefully about how best to organise their financial affairs. Banks and building societies are eager to woo young people, seeing them as lucrative long-term customers. But beware of the freebies and special offers: small depositors generally get the worst deal from the big banks. Open a bank account, by all means, but do not expect it to make much money. If you want to save, try a tax-free account (Tessa) or a Pep/ISA (see questions 13 and 14).

You may be better off using your bank or society as a source of cheaper loans: many deposit-takers offer interest-free loans, and some extend these into your first one or two years in a job. Student credit cards are also available.

One of the least welcome costs for a student is insurance, but a stereo, television, books and clothes should all be covered. Parents can extend their home contents policies, but be sure to check the conditions (see question 21). Some insurers, like Endsleigh, offer policies specially tailored to students, covering everything from bicycles to books. They also cover break-ins at student halls and other accomodation.

Start your career

Once out of university and in the real world, your serious financial planning has to start. You may have debts carried over from your student days and these should be paid off as quickly as possible, which may be painful.

However, one of the first things financial advisers suggest is a pension (see questions 41-50). Retirement may seem a distant prospect but the advantage of starting young is that small amounts of money salted away over many years can lead to a very comfortable retirement, and may even allow you to retire early.

Once a man reaches the age of 30, he would have to make gross monthly contributions of £580 a month to retire at 55, so there is no time to lose.

Now is the perfect time to put other regular savings vehicles into place. Consider a personal equity plan (Peps), either in unit or investment trusts (see question 16) which invests in stocks and shares. These should reap large rewards over the long term, and with so much time to play with, you can afford to try some of the more volatile emerging markets funds that may take many years to develop (see questions 14 and 15).

Shorter term savings should be kept in building societies, since stockmarket investments are risky if invested for any period under five years.

Insurance against illness is also advisable now. Premiums for Personal Health Insurance and Critical Illness (see question 22) will be cheaper the younger you are. These policies pay an income or a lump sum if you are struck with a range of illnesses that prevent you from working.

Young family

Your fourth financial age is perhaps the most complex, financially. Married, or co-habiting, with children or children on the way, young families often have to deal with severe financial strains.

A comfortable home is highest on the list of financial priorities for young families. And with homes, invariably comes a home loan: the mortgage market is littered with a huge array of special deals (see questions 1-10).

You will also want to save, because future costs suddenly loom large with a baby on the way, and perhaps half your income is under threat (since one of you will probably take time off for the baby). Long term savings are better off in a personal equity plan (Pep), a tax-free unit trust that invests in a range of underlying shares, or an ISA, a package of shares, cash deposits and insurance, to replace Peps in April 1999. More cautious people may opt for a tax free building society account (Tessa), which must be held for five years, but are due to end in April 1999 (although Tessas set up before then may run their full terms).

You should be aware, however, that the stock market virtually always outperforms building societies over five years, so see an expert (see questions 11-20).

Life cover — at the very least, term assurance — is essential. You would also be wise to buy some sort of medical insurance (see questions 21-30). And you should be thinking about your pension (see questions 41-50).

Of course, the biggest expense to hit married couples can be when things go wrong and divorce ensues. New laws have been introduced allowing wives a share of their husbands' pension when they divorce (see question 46).

Retirement

Your retirement years could be a blissful time of gardening and sunny cruises. But if you do not plan properly, it is more likely to mean shivering under a blanket in a damp room — Labour has admitted that it cannot afford the £90 billion welfare bill, and may introduce some form of compulsory second-tier pension scheme.

If you have access to a company pension scheme, it is almost always sensible to take it. They vary between final salary schemes, which pay a percentage of your final salary when you retire, and money purchase schemes, which build up a fund of capital which has to be spent on an annuity at retirement (see questions 41- 50).

Annuities simply pay you an income from your capital, based on the insurer's assumption of how long you will live. These days, smokers, highly stressed workers and obese people can get a better annuity rate in retirement.

A pension is not the only consideration. If you are likely to have an estate worth over £223,000 when you die, you may want to exploit the various inheritance tax loopholes, otherwise 40% of everything you own above that amount will go to the government (see questions 31-40).

Planning for long term care is also essential. Labour is expected to assist people who cannot afford long-term care assurance, but exactly how is not yet clear — possibly through a partnership scheme which protects part of your assets if you put some money towards the costs of care.

Buying your home

The Essential Questions:

❓ Is it better to rent or buy?

🅐 Whether to rent or buy your home was not even an issue 10 years ago. Buying was always the preferred option as people begged and borrowed to clamber on to the housing ladder and make a small fortune out of soaring property prices. But times have changed. The 80s may have been a one-way ticket to riches, but the housing market of the 90s has made many people rue the day they bought their home.

Thanks to the housing recession, the rise of negative equity, and more than 300,000 repossessions during the last six years, the number of people choosing to rent has rocketed.

However, the old saying that it is better to buy than to rent is still true, though there are some exceptions.

Broadly, if you cannot afford a deposit or are likely to move house regularly, it is probably better to rent. The costs involved in moving every couple of years could outweigh the savings of a cheap mortgage.

Also remember that if you have to stretch your budget to pay the mortgage, you may not be able to afford a hike in interest rates. Mortgage payments can increase far more rapidly than rental payments, which generally rise in line with inflation.

Renting is also more flexible than buying. You can move at short notice with the minimum of fuss, making it ideal for people whose jobs involve a regular change of location. Nor will you have to maintain the property.

But with a housing recovery well under way, property is getting more expensive again. In fact, the average house has just exceeded its 1989 peak level. If you do not fall into any of the categories above, you should cross hell and high water to secure a mortgage and buy your home.

It is actually cheaper to buy than to rent, and the longer you stay in the property, the bigger the savings.

According to Abbey National, a two-bedroom flat in London would cost almost £170,000 more over 25 years through renting than if you bought. Even on a four-bedroom house in London, renting will cost almost £100,000 more over a 25-year term.

As Europe's most expensive city as far as rents are concerned London may be an extreme example, but the same applies when you look at any major city in the UK.

In terms of affordability, things are getting more expensive. A typical buyer needs to spend about £31 out of every £100 of take-home pay, says C&G.

Then there are the quality-of-life considerations. If you rent, you may not be able to furnish or decorate the property to your own taste, and, although you can still lose your home if you fail to pay the rent, you may be ejected simply because the landlord wants you out. Current rental contracts give the landlord far more rights than the tenant.

Finally there is the abiding logic that you are better off paying for something that you will actually own one day.

Q Which is the best mortgage for me?

A You have finally decided to buy a home. The market is on the rise again, making bargains harder to find.

The furthest thing from your mind may be the type of mortgage to get. But the kind of loan determines how and when you will pay it off. It may be the difference between an easy ride or a nightmare.

There are two main types: repayment and endowment. An endowment mortgage is, in essence, a savings scheme to repay the loan capital at the end of the term. It has enough life assurance to pay off the loan if you die prematurely. Your monthly payments go into a life company's endowment fund, and are then invested in the stock-market and other securities. It may be a traditional with-profits life assurance scheme, which saves profits made in good years to pay out in bad ones, helping smooth your returns; or a unit-linked policy, which follows the ups and downs of the market.

The fund is supposed to grow to pay off the loan at the end of the term, but you pay the interest separately.

Borrowers also receive a bonus at the end of the scheme and an extra lump sum if the policy's profits top the size of your loan. But there is no guarantee, and you could be left with a shortfall instead.

A key advantage is that an endowment policy can be taken with you if you move. And when interest rates are low, the mortgage can be cheaper than a repayment scheme. But endowment mortgages come with high up-front commission fees and charge substantial surrender penalties if you bale out early.

Most experts now agree that a repayment mortgage is more suitable for most people. You simply repay a sum consisting of both capital and interest monthly over the term, typically 25 years. In the early years, you pay mainly interest and later mostly capital.

There are other options. You may prefer a pension or Pep mortgage, which are similar in some ways to an endowment mortgage.

A pension mortgage has advantages for those prepared to use the lump-sum part of their pension to pay off their loan. You meet the interest payments during the term and also pay into a pension fund. The advantage is that you enjoy tax relief on both interest and pension payments. But you need a bigger-than-normal personal pension to do this. Most company pensions cannot be used.

A Pep mortgage is similar. You pay off only the interest during the term, while building a Pep fund to pay off the capital at its end. Pep schemes are very flexible, allowing you to stop contributions in hard times. Endowment schemes, and most pensions schemes, do not allow this. However, with the advent of the individual savings account next year contributions will have to go into your ISA instead, and they have a lower contribution limit of £5,000 a year.

All mortgages enjoy tax-relief (Miras, or mortgage interest relief at source) on the first £30,000 of the loan.

Until 1988, each individual could claim Miras on their own £30,000 share of the mortgage, meaning relief on up to £60,000. It was then changed to £30,000 per household. The relief could still be claimed by unmarried couples after 1988 if they bought their home before the ruling, but if they later wed and did not inform their lender, they may have continued to receive the relief, and could be liable for a hefty back-tax bill if they are found out.

Q How can I get the best mortgage deal?

A Most homebuyers take their mortgages from the building society where they hold their savings account. This does not always make sense: just because you have a savings account with a society does not mean it will offer you the best mortgage deal.

You are better off seeking a bargain elsewhere: the mortgage market is full of discounted, fixed and variable rate loans. There are repayment, endowment, Pep and pension mortgages. And there are special offers, cashbacks and first-time buyers' mortgages (see question 6).

Given such variety, how do you find the best deal?

You could do worse than go to an independent financial adviser (IFA). They haven't got the best reputation as a result of recent scandals, but they do seem to be getting their act together. Be warned, however, that those who advise purely on mortgages should be a member of the Council of Mortgage Lenders Code of Practice. If they are not, then go elsewhere. If they advise on the endowment component, however, they must be regulated by the Personal Investment Authority.

Nevertheless, mortgage advisers offer a convenient snapshot of the best deals on the market, and can save you a lot of money. Ideally, choose a fee-charging adviser. Good fee-charging financial advisers will trawl through every mortgage on the market, and adapt one to your needs. For this service, they will charge £200 to £300.

Mortgage advisers charge borrowers in one of three ways: a flat fee; an introductory commission from the building society the adviser recommends (which is ultimately paid by you, and is about the same price); or a commission from the insurer

level of mortgage advice they can give.

Lloyds/TSB is the only one so far to refuse to sign up the the "third tier" of advice — a specific recommendation of a mortgage. The rest have agreed to all three levels of service, which starts with simply handing out information and progresses to a "shortlist" of loans to choose from, neither of which are much help.

providing the endowment or Pep component of an interest-only loan. Always ask your adviser how much he or she is receiving in commission, and from what source. There are a small number of specialist mortgage brokers, but most advisers sell home loans along with other financial products.

Some advisers are in fact banks and building societies — Bradford & Bingley is one of the biggest independent financial advisers in Britain.

Recently, the banks and building societies have been asked to sign up to a Code of Practice which determines the

Only the specific loan recommendation is really useful but be sure to shop around for several opinions before choosing. And remember to ask about any penalties for early redemption.

Beware of dodgy or risky mortgage deals: the telltale signs are lenders eager to lend more than three and a half times your salary.

Q Should I buy a fixed or variable rate mortgage?

A The choice is a tough one: should you risk a variable rate mortgage, and hope that interest rates come down; or should you go for a fixed rate in the expectation that you will make a saving?

With economists saying that mortgage rates are at or near their peak, averaging 8.7% today, the likelihood that they will fall over the coming years, especially with the need to cut rates to meet the European Monetary Union (EMU) criteria, is very high. But before making the decision, it is worth understanding the difference between fixed and variable rate mortgages.

A variable rate mortgage is one where the interest on your homeloan moves in tandem with the rise and fall in base rates. (The base rate is the lending rate set by the Bank of England on the money it lends. It is usually one or two percentage points lower than the interest charged by banks and building societies — the

difference represents the lenders' profit margins on their loans to the public).

Fixed rates are set at the same level for a pre-determined period, anything from two to twenty-five years. However, the longer you fix for, the greater the chances that the interest rates will fall to below your fixed level, leaving you paying more than everybody else.

With experts agreeing that rates are bound to fall over the next few years, fixing seems foolish at first sight.

But although variable rates have risen by around 20% in the past year, fixed rates remain an attractive option. In addition, a small rise in variable rates is not out of the question, though that may be the last rise before they start falling again.

Advisers say that unless you think variable rates will plummet, then the range of fixed and discounted deals, some as low as 6.25% for five years, and only slightly lower for three years, are the best way forward. Others, however, point to "capped" rates. These will fall if interest rates drop, but are guaranteed not to rise above a pre-determined level if rates rise.

If you think that rates will fall significantly, then discounted rates offer another solution. They are set at varying discounts to the variable rate. If the variable rate falls, so will your discounted rate. If it rises, your monthly repayments will rise too.

However, you are guaranteed never to pay more than the variable rate, so you will not be stranded at a high rate when everybody else is paying less, as could happen with fixed rates. The cheapest discounted deals at the moment are 2.5% off for

three years and 1.35% off for five years. Capped rates are available at between 6.25% and 6.75% for four and five years.

The catch with both fixing and taking a discounted deal are the redemption penalties and tie-in periods that are often attached.

Very often you are required to stay with the lender for two or three years after your fixed or discounted deal has expired, otherwise you face a hefty penalty, usually equivalent to the amount of money you have saved by taking the cheap deal in the first place.

However, if you do take a fixed or discounted deal, and rates do fall, then remaining tied to your lender at the predicted lower variable rates will not be any hardship.

For the wary, either three or five year fixed rates, or capped rates for the same period, seem to be the best option.

ⓠ How large a loan can I afford to take out?

Ⓐ In deciding how big a loan you can afford, heed the lessons of the great property crash of 1989 to 1994. At the height of the 1980s property boom, people were taking out loans worth four or five times their salaries. Those on £20,000 took on £80,000 loans, first-time buyers queued up for 100% mortgages and lenders, released from credit controls, were only too eager to meet the demand. Then interest rates soared to more than 15%, prices crashed and thousands found themselves owning properties worth less than their loan, the so-called negative equity trap. Unable or unwilling to sell, they watched their houses plunge in value.

Homebuyers and lenders seem to have learnt the lessons of that debacle: building societies are reluctant to lend more than three times a salary, and sensible homebuyers are borrowing two to three times their salary at the most. Indeed, a new kind of homebuyer has emerged, one who takes care about how much he or she can afford, especially if interest rates rise.

However, three times your salary is a crude way of calculating how much you can afford to borrow. A single person may easily afford four times salary while a parent with several dependants may only manage one or two times salary.

The best way to calculate the amount you can afford to borrow is to take your net disposable income – total income minus essential outgoings – and calculate how much of it you can afford to spend on repaying your loan. Many mortgage advisers now ask homebuyers to work out their net disposable income before offering a loan.

To do so, follow these easy steps: first, calculate your monthly living expenses, including all bills and outgoings for you and your dependants. Then work out how much of the remaining sum you can afford on repaying your mortgage. A £100,000 repayment loan, for example, will cost about £800 a month at today's rates. If this eats up most of your income after living costs are removed, then it is too expensive.

You need some money left in case interest rates rise. Remember, despite economists predicting interest rates will fall, there is always the chance they have got things wrong.

Also, think about future demands on your income. Are you planning to have children? How secure is your job? If you are self-employed, is your future income safe? In the 1990s, lenders want to know if your income is sustainable over the longer term. Experts warn that the self-employed and those with a poor credit rating may not be offered a loan; it all

depends on recent history, trading figures and evidence of ability to repay the loan.

If you have a six-month work contract, and no trading history, you may have trouble getting a loan. A lender might look for proof that you can save enough to meet an unexpected interest rate rise.

People deemed to be a credit risk will have to reassure societies that their circumstances have changed. It may be worth finding out your credit details before you apply for a loan. Experian, formerly CCN, and Equifax are the biggest credit ratings agencies in Britain, and regularly supply credit details to banks and building societies, who also operate a credit scoring system based on your credit history. A bad credit record can stem from many things, ranging from bankruptcy to failing to pay the council tax. So check out your record if you think it may have a black mark.

Q What are the most innovative homeloans?

A The fierce competition among lenders has spawned a huge array of innovative home loans, tailored to special groups such as first-time buyers, the self-employed and people with negative equity. Even expectant mothers now have their own specially designed mortgages, and some lenders now let you use your mortgage as a current bank account.

Lenders have repackaged their loans to boost the property market, which is continuing to emerge from its worst slump since the war.

The problem is, with so many mortgages on the market, the public is totally bewildered by the more innovative packages available.

So what's on offer? For first-time buyers, a large choice of loans is available. As the market recovers, 100% mortgages are coming back. But beware: hurt by the crash, lenders now regard anyone who borrows 100% of a property's value as a high credit risk. They may impose a higher interest rate as a result.

Experts warn that some silly deals are being offered to first-time buyers. If you are buying for the first time, beware of heavily discounted first-time loans which are cheap in the early years and then jump up to the variable rate. The shock can result in severe repayment pressures unless you are prepared.

Some discounted deals have offered rates as low as 1% for the first year. This may seem amazingly cheap, but again, the shock of jumping back up to the floating rate can be intolerable for many borrowers. Better to go for a more realistic 2-3% discount off the variable rate for, say, three years — keeping in mind the sudden rise later.

Also check the lock-in period: many cheap fixed deals lock you in to the variable rate for three to five years after the fixed period ends, and if rates are high, you will be squeezed without any way out (except by paying a big penalty to the lender, typically six months' interest).

Cashbacks are also a popular innovation – gifts of cash from the lender to tempt first-time buyers and re-mortgagees. They can be worth up to 6% of the loan – about £3,000 on an average mortgage. But they often have heavy conditions attached – so read the small print.

For those with negative equity, loans are available that cover the debt plus the cost of borrowing to buy a new property – thus freeing the borrower from the trap. Lenders are choosy about who should buy a negative-equity mortgage, and many offer them only to their most reliable customers.

The biggest innovation in the market this year is a mortgage that works in a similar way to a current bank account. It allows you to pay off more than you need to, and then use the surplus equity as a cheap way of borrowing to fund other expenditure. For example, you may increase the monthly payments beyond the minimum to service the loan, as a way of saving for the future. Or the extra savings can be used as a form of insurance: to pay the mortgage if you are temporarily out of work or on maternity leave. Some lenders have even issued cheque books and credit cards linked to your mortgage account, so the in-built surplus will allow you to do away with your bank account altogether.

The Halifax and other big lenders are looking closely at the bank-account style of mortgage. But Mortgage Trust and Virgin already offer bank-account type loans. Many believe this is the way of the future for homeloans: as an anchor for your savings, not your debts.

Q If I've got the wrong mortgage, how do I get the right one?

A It is easy to be complacent about your mortgage. Once it is up and running, and the stress of moving house is over, few people want to return to the mind-numbing world of home loans. In fact, many would happily pay slightly over the odds for a continued easy life.

But arranging a cheaper mortgage and saving a small fortune on your monthly mortgage payments involves no more than filling in a couple of forms, and needn't cost you a penny.

Many lenders are offering fee-free deals where they will pay the moving expenses such as legal and valuation fees — but these may not be around for long. However, the interest rate is of prime importance. Read the best mortgage rate tables in The Sunday Times, or speak to a mortgage broker who will endeavour to dig out the best deal for you. Alternatively, ring around a few banks and building societies, tell them you are considering remortgaging and see what they offer.

If they offer a good deal, tell your existing lender you are remortgaging with someone else. This may not get any response at first because your lender may think you are bluffing, but it often ends up with a second, better offer from your own lender to prevent you leaving.

If you have some equity in your property or a large deposit, there are some exceptional variable rates on offer from some of the direct mortgage providers which deal over the phone such as Direct Line, First Direct and Bradford & Bingley Direct.

Alternatively, explore the world of fixed and discounted mortgage rates. These tend to be the most popular choice for people remortgaging to save money. The advantage of discounted deals is that if

best option.

However, there are several pitfalls. Most importantly, if you are currently paying a fixed rate, you will have to pay a penalty fee if you jump ship to another lender. As a rule, the fee is roughly equal to the savings you have made through the fixed rate, giving the lender a chance to recoup rates fall, so will the rate you pay, meaning you cannot get stranded paying high rates when almost everyone else is paying less. It also means that if rates rise, so will your payments, though for the discounted period they will remain lower than the norm.

its losses. It also prevents sharp operators constantly chasing the best rates.

The penalties often apply long after the fixed or discounted deal has expired, so check this out before you move, and also ensure that the variable rate you will revert to after the fixed period has expired is competitive, otherwise the savings will be clawed back very quickly.

With fixed rates, you must be confident that rates will not fall much further because if they do, you will be stuck on the higher rate (see question 4).

With interest rates predicted to fall, many advisers are pointing to cheap fixed or capped rates as the

However, with capped rates, redemption penalties are less of a worry because if rates fall, so will your repayments, and there is no chance of being stranded on a higher rate than everybody else.

Q What should I do if my home has fallen in value?

A Sit and wait is the option chosen by many people. Wait for the house-price recovery to gather more steam, and then sell.

That is all right for people who want to move and whose homes have fallen slightly in value. But the problem is, your home is not a stock to be bought and sold when the price is right. It's where you live, a fact that seemed to elude people in the late 1980s.

In the 1990s, more people understand this, having been burnt by the property crash. So it is unlikely that prices will move upwards at anything like the rate they did in the late1980s — especially in these days of low inflation. Those still in negative equity can expect to be in a more positive situation soon (and certainly their numbers are dwindling rapidly) but perhaps not as quickly as they had hoped.

This recovery is not like the previous housing boom: while experts believe prices may rise by an average of 5% this year, some think that will slow down in 1999.

That said, the move towards monetary union is likely to push interest rates down, and some think a post millenium boom is a real possibility. Certainly, first-time buyers are returning to the market as low interest rates boost affordability.

The long wait has certainly been worth your while if you are one of the estimated 300,000 people still with negative equity. The reason is that in most cases of negative equity, the home loan is worth just a few hundred pounds more than your home. So it should not take long before prices rise to a level that would cover your debt to the lender. If you sell at this time, you cannot hope for

IT COMES FITTED WITH AN AIR BAG IN CASE THERE'S A PROPERTY CRASH

FOR SALE

-PILBROW-

much back on your own equity, of course.

But what if you are desperate to move, or have a large negative-equity problem that is not going to disappear in a hurry? Lenders have come up with special negative-equity packages. These will lend a maximum of 130% on your next property, which would cover a substantial negative-equity gap.

Take a homeowner who wants to move to a £90,000 home, but has an existing mortgage of £60,000 on a home now worth just £50,000. Most negative-equity mortgages will lend £100,000 — covering the debt on the old property (£10,000) plus 100% of the value of the new one. The problem is that such packages are only available to borrowers with an impeccable repayment record and considerable savings.

Lenders are more cautious than ever before, and have even drawn up blacklists of groups who may be unable to finance their loan if things go wrong: the self-employed, very high borrowers, and people in risky industries with high staff turnover.

The most sensible response to a fall in the value of your home can be simply to ignore it. There is little you can do in the short term. If you are prepared to wait, you may eventually make a profit.

Q How can I save my home if I lose my job?

A The world was once a harsher place: if you failed to pay your mortgage, you were often turfed out on to the street. These days, lenders tend to be kinder to borrowers in trouble.

Many societies – especially mutual ones – say they will look sympathetically on any homeowner who alerts them early to a problem with repayments due to job loss or illness.

This is a belated gesture of goodwill; after all, big banks and societies did more than anyone in the 1980s to encourage people to over-extend themselves, by offering 100% loans that were often four or five times the borrower's income. It is worth restating the advice often given: only ever borrow a maximum of three times your income.

Some lenders now even give borrowers with a good chance of getting another job a temporary repayment holiday, but don't count on it.

There are more definite ways of retaining a roof over your head if you lose your job, or suffer an accident or illness. One is to take out an insurance policy.

Lenders stung by repossessions due to rising unemployment are now demanding that new borrowers take out some form of mortgage protection, a vague term meaning different things to different people. Some lenders call such policies accident, sickness and unemployment (ASU) cover; or simply mortgage protection.

But read the small print very carefully: certain policies are merely life assurance designed to repay the mortgage if you die, and have nothing to do with paying your mortgage in the event of job loss or accident.

Proper ASU insurance will cover your mortgage repayments if you fall ill, lose your job, or become disabled through an accident. It normally costs approximately £6 per £100 of debt repayable per month (that is, a premium of £30 a month to cover a £500 monthly mortgage).

However, there are problems with such policies. To start with, they pay out for a maximum of 12 months, and usually don't start paying out until two months after you lose your job (or get ill). So if you get another job or recover within that time, your premiums would have been wasted.

Another option is to rely on the government, through mortgage-interest support schemes. But in October 1995, new rules were introduced.

Under the new regime, mortgage support can be claimed only if you have been out of work, or otherwise unable to pay your mortgage, for nine months, when 100% of the loan costs will be met, but only on loans of up to a maximum of £100,000.

If you have total assets of £8,000 or more you fail to qualify, so only about three out of 10 people are thought to be eligible for government relief.

A third option is to pay more for your mortgage than you need to, thus building up a surplus fund that can be drawn on if you lose your job or fall ill.

Several new mortgages allow you to use your loan as a current account, topping it up when necessary and withdrawing when times are hard. In the case of sickness or disability, your employer may also help.

But there is a lot to be said for co-operating with your lender. If you alert your lender to any problem immediately, most will enter into some arrangement. Common sense suggests you should, wherever possible, avoid missing mortgage payments by setting aside money for a rainy day.

Q How do I go about letting my home?

A Landlords are popularly thought of as gruff and greedy ogres, intent on squeezing their tenants for every penny. No doubt some measure up to the cliché, but an equal number are well-meaning people who simply want to let their homes.

Being a landlord can be harrowing, especially if it is your home being occupied by squatters or careless tenants.

So what's the safest way of becoming a landlord? The first step is to calculate the rental value of your property.

Contact at least two agents, for a valuation.

Next, advertise your property. Experienced landlords recommend going through an agent and not through the papers. Good agents will check thoroughly tenants' references, credit records and any history of arrears. Be sure to use an agent who is a member of the Association of Residential Letting Agents. Some offer insurance policies covering unpaid rents and the legal cost of ejecting sitting tenants.

Agents' commission is set according to the service: to find a tenant, expect to pay 10% of the rent; 12.5% to find the tenant and collect rents; and 15% for a full

management service, useful if you're going abroad.

The rental agreement is crucial: ideally, it should be an assured shorthold tenancy agreement, and you must notify the tenant of the type of agreement at the outset. Failure to do so means the tenant could become a protected or sitting tenant.

An assured shorthold is typically renewable every six months with a two-month notice period on either side. It gives the landlord a legal right to recover his or her property after six months, and the tenant a rolling agreement with a long notice period built in.

If you want to recover your

property, you have to serve two months' notice on your tenant before the six-month period ends: if you miss the deadline by a single day, the tenant, technically, has the right to remain in the property until the next rental-payment date.

Landlords must also be aware of their legal obligations: you must inspect the gas appliances on an annual basis (following a case in which a tenant died when a negligent landlord failed to check the heaters), and keep a close eye on other possible problems that may arise. And you are obliged by law to tell your lender, house insurer and the Inland Revenue of your decision to let your home.

If you, and not your agent, collect the rent, insist on a monthly standing order. Cheques tend to get lost in the post.

Saving and investing

The Essential Questions:

ⓠ What can I learn from the world's greatest investors?

Ⓐ A great deal. But remember: the greatest investors are not geniuses or rocket scientists. They are pragmatic people who stick to a few fundamental investment truths. Their main distinguishing feature is nerves of steel.

Take Sir John Templeton, the legendary founder of Templeton Funds, who is today worth about £300m. His guiding principle is to invest at the time of maximum pessimism. Buying when stockmarkets were at their lowest then selling when they rose to a peak helped turn a £10,000 investment in the Templeton Growth Fund in 1954 into more than £1.42m today.

Few ordinary investors have the confidence to invest during a recession. They make the big mistake of ploughing into the stockmarket when prices are at an all-time high, during a boom. Indeed, the collapse of every bull market — when shares rise fastest — has been heralded by a bout of frenzied share buying by ordinary investors. Many won't have bought a share in their lives, get badly burnt, and pull-out until a top-heavy bull-market tempts them in again.

So timing is crucial. A master of long-term investment timing was the late tycoon, Sir James Goldsmith, whose net worth was estimated at £1.15bn. He successfully anticipated the financial crash of 1974 and sold his shares, bought ahead of the boom of the early 1980s, and sold well before the great stockmarket crash of 1987, when shares lost a third of their value. His strategy is to second guess the effect on share prices of a change in economic direction or government policy.

Most of us do not have the information to invest in Goldsmith's way. But don't

worry: the greatest investors of all ignore big economic questions altogether; they focus on the fundamental value of solid companies.

America's Warren Buffett is the world's most spectacular example of a "value-driven" investor: he has outperformed the US index of leading shares in every year since 1956. To do this he uses four basic steps: "Switch off the stock-market" – ignore wild price movements and keep faith in fundamental value, regardless of market sentiment; "forget about the economy" – waste no time analysing interest rates, debt and inflation and concentrate simply on compa-nies that will grow regardless of bad economic conditions; "understand the business you're buying" – Buffett never invests in anything he cannot understand (no won-der his best buys were Coca-Cola and Gillette); "invest for the long term" – Buffett rarely dumps a stock, and has held some for 30 years.

George Soros's approach is more akin to rocket science. Soros runs the £12bn Quantum Fund which has turned £1,000 invested in 1969 to more than £2m. He made £1bn by selling sterling just after it was ejected from the European exchange rate mechanism. His knack is to second guess the great shifts and swerves of share prices as they react to economic or political change.

Q What should I do with my spare cash?

A You have two main options, assuming you already have the essential insurance cover to support any dependants when you die. Beyond that, you have to decide whether to save or pay off your debts.

Paying off debts might not sound very exciting but at certain times, when the cost of borrowing is higher than the rate of inflation, it is arguably the most astute thing to do with your spare cash.

At times when inflation is higher than interest rates, on the other hand, repaying debts can be given a low priority because inflation will be eroding the real value of the debt more quickly than interest is adding to it.

With inflation at about 3% — well below the level of base interest rates — using spare cash to pay off debts should be a high priority.

With interest rates on credit cards, overdrafts and loans sometimes exceeding 25%, reducing your high-interest borrowings is absolutely essential.

You may also want to increase your mortgage repayments, or save lump sums to pay off the capital. This can save thousands of pounds over the term of the mortgage and pay off the debt more quickly. Some lenders are more co-operative than others on this score, so talk to your bank or building society about how you can speed up your mortgage repayments.

Once you have minimised your borrowings, you can concentrate on savings. Exactly where and how you save depends on your timescale and your attitude to risk.

To increase your number of options, you should first ensure you have some instantly accessible savings in a building society to cover any unexpected expenses. You will then be free to consider investments that require a longer-term view.

There are countless options for regular savers, ranging from the building society to stocks and shares, and even emerging-markets unit trusts, which invest in the volatile markets of fledgling economies around the world.

If you can afford to take a five-year view, then you can safely look to stocks and shares to give you the best returns. There has only been one five-year period since the war when shares have not beaten deposit accounts.

Regular savings into unit or investment trusts are exciting and relatively simple. They can also be tax-efficient if you invest through a personal equity plan (Pep) or, from next April, individual savings accounts (ISAs), which pay out all growth and income tax-free.

Pep savings schemes can be started with as little as £25 a month, and there are hundreds to choose from.

The simplest are tracker funds, offered by companies including Richard Branson's Virgin Direct, Fidelity, Legal & General and HSBC, which owns Midland Bank.

These funds simply replicate the performance of a chosen index, usually the FT-SE 100 or the FT-SE-A All-Share. They are easy to monitor (the performance of the indices is reported in the newspapers every day) and extremely flexible, allowing you to reduce or increase your monthly contributions when your circumstances change.

However, the value of your money can go down as well as up, and although over the longer term stocks and shares usually do better than deposit accounts, if you need your money in the short term, you should opt for less volatile, lower-risk savings schemes.

Q Where is my money going to be safe?

A There are a vast number of low-risk investments to choose from, some requiring lump sums, others suitable for regular savings and some that can cater for both.

The key point to remember about risk is that it is not so much dictated by the nature of the investment as by the amount of time you have to play with. Shares are technically risky because in the short term their prices can plummet, but the longer you can wait, the less risky they become.

There has only been one five-year period in Britain since 1945 during which returns on the stockmarket did not outstrip interest paid on cash deposits. However, if you do not have much time to play with and you cannot afford any fluctuations in value, then you must look at the safer, less volatile options.

At the very bottom of the risk scale are National Savings products. These are backed by the government, so, short of the government going bankrupt, you are guaranteed not to lose your money. There is a great range to choose from. Many advisers favour the index-linked savings certificates which offer protec-

tion from increases in the cost of living, promising to pay 2.5% above the rate of inflation for a five-year period.

For non-taxpayers, National Savings income bonds offer good value, paying interest every month at 6.25% gross for investments exceeding £25,000 or 5.5% on at least £2,500 (as at April 1998). The Pensioners Guaranteed Income Bond pays a fixed rate of 7%, but is liable to tax and is only for people aged 60 or over.

Next up the risk ladder are bank and building society accounts. These offer plenty of security but no prospect of capital growth. Society accounts are fine for people requiring an income from

their savings who want to take no risk, though if you are a taxpayer, a tax exempt special savings account (Tessa) is the most sensible option. Average 60-day notice accounts are paying around 6%, while Tessas, which require you to tie your money up for five years, are paying between 7.5% and 8.00% (tax-free). Tessas will cease to accept new deposits from April 1999, although existing schemes will be allowed to run their full term. You can, from that date, put £1,000 per year tax-free into the new ISA accounts.

Government-issued gilts come next in order of risk. Most have a fixed redemption date. If you hold them until maturity there is no risk and you know exactly how much money you will get. But if you want to sell out before maturity, there is a risk you will lose money because the price varies according to the attractiveness of the yield. If the yield looks good compared with the interest rate at the time, the price of the gilt will rise. If it offers poor value, the price will fall.

Or you might try a guaranteed equity plan which offer stockmarket-linked returns, but promise the return of the capital after a fixed period — typically five years.

Q How can I invest for medium risk?

A Once you have taken the big step into medium-risk investments, you must be prepared to take a few knocks on the chin. Medium-risk vehicles usually have the scope to perform like high-risk ones, shooting rapidly up or down in value; but the chances of that happening are not as great as with out-and-out high-risk options.

Remember too, as we said in question 13, the real issue about risk is timescale. A lot of equity investments will be medium-risk over five years but high-risk over one.

Generally speaking, however, it is perfectly possible to invest in the stockmarket in medium-risk unit trusts, though the extent of their riskiness depends on what they invest in.

Emerging markets funds, which invest in the volatile economies of South America and the Far East, are certainly not for the fainthearted. UK and European funds are generally far more stable.

At the low to medium-risk end of the scale are UK tracker funds, offered by Virgin, Fidelity, HSBC, Legal & General and Gartmore, among others. They simply replicate the performance of a chosen index like the FT-SE 100, holding a broad spread of company shares, thereby minimising severe ups and downs. Tracker funds are a safe bet — most "active" fund managers underperform the index. But remember, when the market falls, the index falls with it.

Most growth and income unit trusts will also fall into the medium-risk category, especially over five years.

Growth funds invest with the simple aim of achieving as much capital growth as possible, often targeting under-valued stocks to benefit from rebounds in their share price.

Income funds are targeted at those who need to draw

I SHOULD JUST HAVE INVESTED IN PROPERTY LIKE MY BROTHER

– PILBROW –

an income from their investments, and although many offer fairly low starting yields, sometimes around 3%, they usually manage to increase the amount of income paid over time as the value of the underlying holdings increases, making them ideal hedges against inflation.

However, even investors who do not need any income may consider income funds, as they can sometimes outperform growth funds if the income is reinvested.

They are offered by all the major fund management groups though among the best performers in 1997-98 were Jupiter, Credit Suisse and GT.

Also moderately risky are bonds issued by life insurance companies that invest in the stockmarket.

Included here are with-profits bonds, which smooth the peaks and troughs of the stockmarket by holding back some of the profits from good years to pay out in bad ones.

However, there can be severe penalties if you want to withdraw your money before the end of the bond's term, so be sure you can afford to commit your money before investing.

❶ What are the riskiest investments?

A The short answer is a roulette wheel, a racehorse or a pack of cards. But the investment world has its fair share of extreme risks, and here, like horseracing, one person's risk is another's relaxation.

Risk is also a measure of likely loss. In one sense, the National Lottery is the riskiest investment because the odds of winning the jackpot are 14 million to 1. But the loss is so meagre that most people don't mind it.

Most experts agree that the riskiest investment available to small investors is a warrant fund, the price of which can rise at a tremendous pace then fall back with devastating effect. The reason is that warrants, which give the owner the right to buy shares at a set price, can be traded in their own right, independent of the shares to which they are linked. So they provide exposure to shares at a fraction of the shares' cost, rising and falling far more dramatically than the underlying share. Anyone without nerves of steel should avoid them. For example, Schroders' Japanese Warrant Fund has been one of its most volatile products. It has seen extraordinary ups and downs in recent years because the Japanese market has been on a rollercoaster ride.

The next riskiest investment is a single country emerging market fund. These are unit trusts or investment trusts that invest in shares listed in a single, developing country. Examples are funds investing in China, Thailand, Indonesia, Latin American and east European countries — all very volatile economies.

Such funds are sold by emerging market experts like Schroders, Perpetual, Foreign & Colonial, Templeton and Flemings. Anyone can buy them, for as little as £50 a month. The most exotic emerging market fund manager is Beta Funds, which manages the Gran Caribe Fund (investing in Cuban companies) and two Vietnam funds. But the riskiest of all must surely be the Russian Frontier Trust.

If you want a safer exposure to emerging markets try a fund investing in a spread of markets. There are several emerging market Asian funds that invest in shares quoted in, say, Thailand, Malaysia and Korea; or Latin American funds, investing across Argentina, Chile and Brazil. It is wise to invest no more than 5% of your portfolio in them.

Next down the risk-ranking are general overseas funds, investing in, say, America, Japan and Australia, because there is still a currency risk even though the equity risk is not nearly as great as emerging markets. If you hold shares in dollars, the rate may move against sterling. So even though the share price may rise, your profit may be cut by an adverse exchange rate.

Smaller investors should not get too involved in futures and options, where the risks can be extreme. Futures are normally dealt only by large institutions or very sophisticated and wealthy private investors.

Options are more familiar: they give you the right to buy or sell a share at a pre-agreed price within a set period. So you may, for example, buy an option to buy British Gas shares at 20p in three months' time: if the share rises before then to 40p, then you obviously double your money by buying it at 20p.

Similarly you can buy an option to sell a share in the future, in the hope that its share price falls. Options, however, are quite expensive contracts, so you should weigh the possible gains against the costs of making the transaction.

❶ Which is best — a unit or investment trust?

Ⓐ This is a minefield of misunderstanding, and can end in tears if investors do not fully appreciate the differences between the two.

Although they are both collective investments which invest in a broad spread of stocks and shares (and can both be "pepped" or, from April 1999, wrapped in an ISA), the way they make their profits or losses, and the risks involved, differ radically. To understand why, you have to understand how they work.

A unit trust is a pooled fund of investors' money that is invested in stocks and shares. It is like handing a friend a stack of cash and asking him to invest it for you (for a small fee). If the shares he buys rise in value, you will make money. If they fall, you will lose. It is as simple as that.

Investment trusts are more complicated. They are publicly quoted companies in their own right, the sole business of which is investing in other stocks and shares. Investors buy shares in the investment trust, which are traded on the stockmarket like any other share. Because share prices are dictated by supply and demand, investment trust shares can rise and fall in value independently, regardless of the value of the stocks and shares held by the trust.

Investment trusts, therefore, offer two ways of making gains or losses: an increase or decrease in the value of the underlying shares, or movements in the share price of the investment trust itself. Investment trusts also differ from unit trusts because many have a fixed life, typically 10 years. At maturity they are wound up, the underlying shares sold, and the proceeds handed back to investors. Some have no wind-up date and carry on trading ad infinitum.

The value of the portfolio of shares held by the trust is known as the trust's net asset value, or NAV. If demand for the investment trust is high because investors think its outlook is good, the share price will rise above the value of the underlying shares — ie, it is said to trade at a "premium" to net asset value. If demand is low, the opposite occurs and, like many investment trusts, trades at a "discount" to NAV. For example, shares in the Dartmoor investment trust, run by Exeter Fund Managers, were trading at a 12.4% premium to NAV in March 1998 because demand was high. Conversely, shares in the Fleming Asian investment trust were trading at a 20% discount because demand was low.

Many investors make a lot of money by buying into investment trusts when they are trading at a discount and waiting for the discount to narrow, either when sentiment about that trust improves, or when it approaches its maturity date and everybody knows that the full NAV will soon be distributed.

Making a choice between investment and unit trusts is tricky.

Some fund managers have identical unit and investment trusts, which are run by the same person and which invest in the same stocks. When the investment trust is trading at a premium, the equivalent unit trust is the obvious choice and vice versa.

Investment trusts often outperform unit trusts in the longer term. For one thing, they have lower charges. And they are allowed to borrow money to expand their portfolio. That is why, when the stockmarket is rising, an investment trust performs better than a unit trust. However, if the stockmarket falls, investment trusts can be hit harder.

❓ How do I know which are the best shares to buy?

A If we knew which shares to buy we would not be sitting here trying to answer this question. We would be thinking up ways of spending our fortune.

Nobody knows exactly which shares are going to perform. But there are proven ways to make a calculated guess.

You should first understand a little about how the stockmarket works. Basically, share prices rise when there are more buyers than sellers in the market: if there is strong demand for a particular company, its shareprice goes up, as investors outbid each other for the stock (in the same way bidders at an auction drive up the price of a lot). By the same principle, a share price falls when there are more sellers than buyers of the stock.

Obviously, you should buy shares you believe are likely to rise before others decide to buy them.

The best advice is to find shares that you think are undervalued. In other words, companies with share prices lower than you think they deserve to be, given the com-pany's prospects. The most common measure of future profitability is the prospective price/earnings ratio. This is the price per share divided by the company's anticipated future earnings per share. It is shown in most newspapers' share tables. A company with a p/e of 10 is said to be trading at ten times earnings.

Normally, a high p/e ratio means investors expect a company's profits will grow more strongly than those of a company with a low p/e. A company trading at 30 or 40 times earnings may be overvalued, and probably a sell, while one trading at 15 times earnings, undervalued and therefore a buy. So look for companies with a low rating that you think should be higher. A rather dull

We're all on prozac, but she's got shares in it as well.

company may be trading at only 5 to 10 times earnings. But let's say you find out something about the company: it has a new product or a dynamic new executive. Suddenly, its p/e looks unjustifiably low, since its earnings are likely to rise as a result.

But the p/e is just one measure of value. You should also check a number of other factors, including: the company's earnings per share history; the return on shareholders' equity; cash flow (check that operating cash flow is better than operating profit); and whether the company has a strong balance sheet. If in doubt, ask a stockbroker.

Many people buy shares to receive an income through annual dividend payments, rather than take a gamble on a rise in share prices.

Income-producing shares tend to be low risk, blue chip stocks like Shell, BP, the privatised utilities, and British Airways.

A final word: remember that every expert is fallible. Even the greatest investors get it wrong. So trust your judgment – if you come up with an idea based on your own "gut feel" – bounce it off a stockbroker.

Some of the best ideas are all around you: the board game that was a huge hit over Christmas; the airline with the best service; the computer software game that children love to play: find out the names of the companies behind these products.

And before plunging in, do your research. It may be worth running a fantasy portfolio for a while, to see how your choices work in safety.

Q Can I put my money offshore?

A The answer is yes, but only if you are fully aware of the risks and only within strict parameters. Offshore literally means anywhere outside Britain. But technically it has come to mean anywhere beyond the reach of the UK taxman. New Labour cracked down on investing offshore in several ways in its 1998 budget.

The most popular way to invest offshore is in a fund based in tax havens such as Jersey, Guernsey, The Isle of Man, Luxembourg and Dublin. Here, they escape UK taxes and are comparatively free from regulations. They may be distributor funds, where income must be distributed — and are taxed if received in the UK; or roll-up funds, where the income is not realised until the assets are sold.

If you are living overseas, it makes sense to invest in an offshore fund, because you avoid paying tax on the income and capital gains while you are living outside Britain. British residents, too, can invest in offshore funds. They must, however, declare their holdings on their tax return because they are obliged to pay tax on their worldwide assets. Higher-rate tax payers can defer and even avoid tax by investing in a roll-up fund in the years before retirement. Payment of tax on assets otherwise taxable at 40% can be deferred until after they retire, when the proceeds will be taxable only at the lower rate of 20%. But the budget tightened up this loophole.

Offshore funds tend to mirror their UK counterparts in terms of where they invest. But they have wider powers to buy riskier securities as well. There is a full range investing in mainstream markets — Britain, America, Europe and Japan — and many that invest in more exotic locations, including emerging markets.

But there are crucial differences. Their pricing structure is simpler than UK unit trusts. They often have a single buying and selling price from which the initial charge and administration fee is deducted and clearly stated (unlike UK unit trusts, which still apply a complicated bid-offer spread between the buy and sell prices, which tends to hide the charges).

They usually charge more than domestic funds — often 5% to 7% initially, with a 1% to 2% annual fee. The reason is they can invest more widely and can be denominated in any currency.

Other ways of investing offshore were severely curtailed in the 1998 budget. The main targets were people retiring abroad, the UK-based beneficiaries of offshore trusts, those with high foreign earnings, and holders or personal portfolio bonds.

In particular, the budget outlawed the practice of avoiding CGT by moving abroad for a short period to redeem foreign-held assets. Now, non-residents will be liable for CGT unless they remain overseas for at least five tax years.

Offshore trusts were hammered in the budget: their tax liabilities will be charged to UK beneficiaries if the settlor (the person who established the trust) is beyond the reach of the Inland Revenue. Previously, UK beneficiaries escaped tax on an offshore trust because the charge fell on the settlor — who was based offshore, and beyond the reach of the UK taxman.

Entertainers, pilots, oil rig workers and anyone with substantial foreign earnings will be hit by the abolition of the foreign earnings deduction. This allowed them to escape UK tax on foreign income if they worked abroad for a qualifying period of 365 days.

Q What will the new ISAs mean for me?

A ISA stands for individual savings account, a tax-free savings plan that will replace Peps and Tessas from April 1999. There is no lifetime limit on how much you can invest in an ISA, however strict annual limits will apply.

For example, you will be able to contribute a maximum of just £5,000 each year into an ISA, compared with £10,800 in a combination of Peps and Tessas.

Like Peps and Tessas, ISAs will be free from income and capital gains tax. But unlike Peps and Tessas, ISAs will not be able to claim the 20% tax credit on dividend payments enjoyed by its predecessors, because the Chancellor has decided to phase this out: for the first five years, ISAs will receive a 10% tax credit on dividends received, and after that, no tax credit at all.

ISAs will be made up of three components – cash, equities and life assurance. So you may wish to use your ISA as a tax-free bank acount (like a Tessa) or as a tax-free unit trust (like a Pep).

You may, alternatively, invest in all three options, so long as you stay within your annual

investment limit. For the first year this will be £7,000, of which no more than £3,000 may be in cash and no more than £1,000 in life assurance schemes. After that the annual contribution limit drops to £5,000, incorporating a £1,000 cash limit.

ISAs will be available from banks, building societies, insurers and investment managers, as well as supermarkets, post offices and National Savings. You can pick one company to run all three elements of your account, or you can select a manager for your share portfolio and a different manager for your cash account.

How much will ISAs cost? Charges for equity ISAs will be

similar to Pep charges, so expect to pay an initial charge of up to 6% and an annual fee of about 1%. If your ISA is a little more than a deposit account, charges will probably be worked into the interest rate, although some providers may levy an annual fee.

You can withdraw money from your ISA at any time without penalty (unlike Tessas, which tied up your money for five years), but once you hit your annual maximum, you cannot make any further contributions, regardless of how much may have subsequently been withdrawn.

You will not be able to switch your Pep directly into an ISA in April 1999; instead, your existing Peps will simply carry on as separate tax-free holdings. While you will be able to change your Pep manager at any time, you will not be allowed to contribute any more money to your Peps.

Tessas taken out before April 1999 will be allowed to run their full five-year term; but after that date, no new Tessas will be allowed.

Q How can I save for my children?

A Putting money aside for your kids is usually a long-term game so the options are incredibly wide, incorporating everything from children's bank and building society accounts to endowment policies and stocks and shares. There is even a Rupert the Bear unit trust run by fund manager Invesco. But do not let the name sway you — it has not done very well and there are plenty of better performing unit trusts available.

Many financial advisers recommend as their first, low-risk choice the National Savings Children's Bonds. They were paying a guaranteed 6% a year tax free in March 1998, but they have to be held for the full five-year term. Anyone over 16 can buy them for anybody under 16. The disadvantage is the lack of immediate access to the money.

If access is important to you, look to the children's bank and building society accounts. These are full of gimmicks like free T-shirts and lunch boxes, but try to concentrate on the interest rate — which can vary widely.

Friendly societies are another option. They allow £25 a month to be invested, with all gains tax free. However, because the investment level is low, charges can be high.

With-profits endowments are another good option for risk-wary parents. They save up gains on the stockmarket and pay them out each year as bonuses, smoothing any peaks and troughs. Once paid they cannot be taken away, so you cannot lose the lot in a stockmarket crash. You do need to be disciplined though — once started, you have to keep paying the premiums for the entire term. If you back out early, the hefty redemption penalties could destroy your gains.

Unit trusts are more flexible. They do not have the with-profits safety net, but

over the long term, it should not be needed. There are more than 1,500 different funds to choose from, ranging from low-risk index tracking funds to volatile emerging markets schemes. Minimum investments range from £20 or £30 a month and over the long term, the benefits of drip-feeding money into trusts can be huge. If you had saved £30 a month into the average UK unit trust for the past 20 years, you would now have more than £38,000.

These investments are also ideal for use in planning for school fees. There are many packaged school fees products, but the packaging can cost a fortune.

Why not buy them a few premium bonds? Minimum investment is £100 and the idea of winning prizes — especially of up to £1m — is appealing to all kids.

As for tax, the situation on children's accounts and investments is wide open to abuse by parents. But beware, the Inland Revenue is watching you.

Children have their own personal allowance of £4,300 from 5 April 1998, which means they can earn that amount in interest before they become liable to tax. So top up their savings, and you can reduce your tax liability.

Insurance

The Essential Questions:

Q What insurance is essential?

A You might think insurance is more of a luxury than a necessity but there are a raft of policies that are essential because the law demands it, your mortgage lender requires it or you would be plain daft not to have it.

The most obvious is motor insurance. Everybody knows that it is illegal to drive without it. Get caught and you will find yourself in court facing a hefty fine and six penalty points on your licence.

If you have a mortgage on your home, you will have to pay for buildings insurance to rebuild your property if it burns down. If you fully own your property and still do not have buildings cover, you are simply mad. Could you afford to rebuild your home?

However, times have changed. It used to be that lenders could force you to take their insurance policies with their mortgage. Not surprisingly, they took advantage of the situation and started charging extortionate premiums. But the stranglehold was broken and you are now entitled to shop around to find the best value.

Even so, many people simply do not bother, and take the policy offered by their lender. Sensible borrowers will refuse.

You will need a life assurance policy if you have a mortgage to pay off the loan if you die. If you have an endowment mortgage, do not worry. The life assurance element will cover the loan. But if you have a repayment or Pep mortgage, you will need a separate term assurance policy to cover your debt. The cheapest providers are Equitable Life, Eurolife and Virgin.

One word of warning: before you take out a policy check whether the premiums are fixed or if the insurer can increase them.

Travel insurance is not a legal requirement. If you have an all-risks home contents policy, it will cover your baggage but not medical expenses. The consequences of not taking out medical cover and then getting injured or falling ill abroad are dire. The cost of treatment on the Continent, the USA, or an air ambulance can run into tens of thousands. Compare this to the cost of a typical annual travel policy of about £90, or less than £50 for a single holiday.

Much like buildings policies sold by mortgage lenders, the travel industry has taken advantage of customer apathy. It is usually offered as part of a package but can be far more expensive than separate, stand-alone schemes. In fact, holidaymakers are better off refusing the agent's offer and buying their own policy. They are available from most banks and building societies, plus specialist insurers.

❶ What insurance is desirable?

Ⓐ You can insure your dog, CD-player, boat or clothes. You can buy cover against the risk of a multiple birth. Ballerinas can insure their feet, violinists their fingers. Burger eaters can even insure themselves against CJD, the human equivalent of mad cow disease.

Many insurance policies are available, but few are truly desirable. We recommend that you consider the following cover, after you have paid for essential policies (see question 21).

• Home contents: covers the contents of your home against fire, theft and other risks. Some policies also cover clothing, cycles and sports equipment, money and credit cards, regardless of whether they are in the home when lost. High-value items such as antiques or jewellery should be insured by specialists such as Hiscox. Garden ornaments may also need separate cover.

• Permanent health insurance: pays out an income until you retire should you suffer a disability rendering you unable to work. Many companies offer this protection through group schemes.

• Private medical insurance: for people who want rapid, quality medical care at any time. Many companies offer private medical insurance as a staff perk. Premiums have risen in recent years but you can cut the cost by excluding outpatient treatment or agreeing to use your policy only for emergencies or major surgery.

• Personal accident insurance: provides a lump sum payable on death, permanent disability or varying degrees of incapacity, where a scale of benefits is applied.

• Accident, disability and unemployment insurance: protects, for example, mortgage payments against any of these eventualities. Typical cover is available up to £1,000 a month. Many people insure up to 125% of their mortgage payment to provide benefits for up to a year.

• Family income benefit: pays out a regular income to your dependants should you die within a specified period. This could cover the period when children are young and perhaps there are school fees.

• Long-term care insurance: one in five people who reaches retirement will need long-term residential care, up to a cost of £20,000 or more a year. So you may well need long-term care insurance.

The government has proposed a much-criticised partnership scheme, where it will match the policyholders' cover on a pound-for-pound basis or more. But that is not yet law and unlikely to become so for some time. In the meantime, there are two types of long-term care insurance: regular premiums, which go up the older you get; or a lump sum investment, which can be used to cut inheritance tax as well as protect savings.

• Critical illness insurance: pays out a lump sum to help cover lost income and costs of treating cancer, heart disease and other serious illnesses. There is a huge range of contracts, so seek independent financial advice. One innovative scheme is Scottish Provident's Self-Assurance range, which offers death and critical illness cover within one plan.

• Homecare emergency service insurance: covers domestic crises such as burst pipes and broken boilers. Green Flag and the AA both offer home cover schemes.

Remember to seek expert financial advice before choosing medical and health-related policies, which are complicated and can have many hidden clauses.

Few people need the full range of "desirable policies" — the choice depends on your circumstances, age and health.

Ⓠ When should I use an insurance broker?

Ⓐ Insurance brokers have had a tough time recently. They have been maligned as unnecessary middlemen who are unable to compete with the direct operators such as Direct Line. There is some truth in this, but only in relation to average customers who simply want a standard policy. In these cases, direct operators are almost always cheaper, because they sell ready-made policies which cater to most of the population.

The disparity between low-risk customers and those viewed as higher risk is widening all the time. Insurers use sophisticated systems to evaluate the risk of particular cars or houses, and direct operators are able to cut costs by refusing cover to those high-risk groups. There are fears that this is leading to the creation of an uninsurable underclass.

In the high-risk circumstances a broker becomes invaluable. If you deviate from the norm in any way, it is usually the insurance broker who comes to the rescue with a suitable and affordable policy.

They work by trawling through the insurance market to identify and negotiate deals for particular groups with particular needs.

This may mean approaching Lloyd's syndicates who offer "niche" products. If you want your spouse and children on your motor policy, for example, or you need special home-contents insurance to cover particularly valuable possessions, a broker will be able to help.

It may be possible to find your own special policies from general insurance companies but going through a broker can save time and money because they often negotiate special discounts for their customers.

Brokers work for all kinds of insurance other than life

products, which are sold by independent financial advisers. Just about every other type of insurance can be bought through a broker — they offer cover for boats, works of art, sports injuries and dangerous holidays.

Brokers claim their value lies not only in finding deals for "non-standard risk" customers but also in their back-up service.

In the event of a claim, the broker will assist you, advising on how best to ensure the biggest payout. Brokers have no interest in scaling down your claim or preventing a payment — they make no money by reducing the size of your claim (direct insurers, on the other hand, need to keep their payouts to a minimum).

Such assistance makes good business sense for brokers because it helps cement customer relationships and engender loyalty.

Brokers are also independent. They can pick and choose from every insurer on the market rather than offering the policies of only one company. Given that no company can be the cheapest and provide the best value all the time, the ability to choose from a wide range makes sense.

They can also give advice on the most suitable policy. In areas such as health cover, this can be invaluable because the policies differ greatly and are littered with exclusions and get-out clauses.

If you value face-to-face contact, you may prefer a broker. They can do business over the phone or will happily sit down with you to discuss your options.

The British Insurance and Investment Brokers Association can provide a list of your local brokers. Or if you want a financial adviser, who deals mostly in life assurance and investments, contact IFA Promotion (see contact numbers at the back).

Q Should I buy financial products direct?

A Yes, if you are a reasonably healthy person with uncomplicated financial affairs and an unblemished past. Direct providers specialise in simple, low-cost policies for low-risk people. Direct insurers, mortgage-lenders and other financial product providers operate simply by taking down your details on the phone and sending you the policy or contract.

Companies such as Direct Line, Virgin and First Direct have stormed the mass market in recent years and have grabbed swathes of business from financial advisers and branch networks of banks and building societies.

If you want a bank account, motor or home insurance, simply get on the phone to one of the direct providers such as Virgin, Direct Line and First Direct. Virgin, for example, will take down your details and a few days later your policy will arrive on your doorstep. All you have to do is sign on the dotted line.

You can also buy a mortgage, personal loan or even a pension through direct providers. The great advantage of going direct is the saving. Because they avoid the overheads of branch networks, direct providers can pass on savings to customers in the form of cheaper premiums, lower mortgage rates and higher investment rates.

Virgin is one of the cheapest providers of term assurance; First Direct one of the most cost-efficient banks and Direct Line and Bradford & Bingley Direct among the cheapest providers of mortgages. Direct Line and Prospero offer among the most competitive standard motor policies.

Low-cost, simple personal pensions sold by telephone are also coming on-stream. The cheapest are offered by Eagle Star, Virgin, Equitable Life, Colonial Direct and

Scottish Widows. Direct pensions for wealthier people, with more sophisticated investment strategies are available from fund managers such as Flemings.

The savings of going direct are substantial. Consider Direct Line, for example. It charges just 7.94% for a mortgage. There is no arrangement fee and no mortgage-guarantee premium and it refunds the valuation fee. As a result, the company's 100 sales people produce £50m to £60m in business a month — an unheard of volume at a society branch.

The advantage of going direct is that what you see is what you get: a simple, cheap, no-frills product. However, there is little or no advice on other options or the more complex insurance savings schemes such as with-profit endowments. Insurance sold direct is merely term cover, with no savings element. Direct mortgages are simple repayment schemes; if you want an endowment attached, go elsewhere.

One of the great advantages of going direct is the time saved: it takes 16 minutes on average for Direct Line to process a mortgage. You can phone from the comfort of your home, and you are always in control of the transaction. And by by-passing the financial adviser, you obviously avoid paying a commission or fee.

❓ How do I protect my home and property?

A There are two principal household insurance policies — buildings and contents. Neither is strictly compulsory but both are more or less essential.

Buildings insurance protects the bricks and mortar of your home and any fitted fixtures within, such as bathroom fittings and built-in cupboards. If the property is damaged by flood, fire or various other perils, the policy pays for repairs.

When you arrange buildings insurance you need to decide on a "sum assured". This is the amount the insurance company would pay out if your home were destroyed. It should be the best estimate of the rebuilding costs and not the market value of the property. You can find out the correct sum assured from the survey when you bought your house. But make sure it is reviewed regularly to take into account rising prices.

Most mortgage lenders make buildings insurance a condition for the loan. They will also try to sell you their own policy — and penalise you if you buy cover elsewhere. Lenders are perfectly within their rights to charge an "administration fee" (usually £25) if borrowers make their own arrangements.

Buildings insurance is a competitive market and the competition is driving prices down. There are hundreds of product providers to choose from. Banks, building societies, insurance brokers and companies that sell direct are all keen to pocket your premiums.

A word about subsidence: the number of claims has risen. Insurers have responded by imposing stiff "excesses" on subsidence claims. The excess is the amount the policyholder is expected to pay towards the costs and it can be as high as £5,000.

With home contents insur-

ance, you also need to decide on a sum assured. You should make a list of all your belongings and the cost of their replacement. But remember that if you underestimate to keep the premium down, you may find that you cannot cover your loss.

Some insurers get around the problem of under-insurance with bedroom-rated policies. This means that houses with a certain number of bedrooms are insured for a certain amount. You may have to list valuable items separately. Each company has its own definition of valuable, but it usually includes hi-fi sets, jewellery and antiques.

Contents policies cover a wide range of perils such as fire and water damage, but premiums are determined by the risk of theft in your area. Insurers offer discounts to policyholders who install alarms and other security devices. Some insist on it.

There are two main types of contents cover. The costlier is "new for old." It simply replaces your old items with new ones. "Replacement" cover is cheaper because it deducts for wear and tear before the claim is settled.

❓ I need car insurance – how do I go about it?

A It may seem straightforward, but these days buying motor insurance can be a complex business. There are so many deals available and several ways of tweaking your premiums or preserving your no-claims discount (NCD).

One thing is certain: third-party motor insurance is compulsory. Everyone must insure against the cost of demolishing another car or causing injury or death to another road user. Third-party rates vary widely depending on the make of the car and a myriad of other factors – age, sex, postcode and so on. Ring several car insurers and ask for quotes.

The complexities arise when you seek comprehensive insurance to cover your own car against damage. Again, the premiums vary hugely. They are set according to your "risk profile"; a young man with an expensive sports car can expect to pay a fortune.

At the other end of the scale is the woman over 50 driving a Reliant Robin. Age, sex, health and postcode – and the car's engine capacity – may all affect the final premiums. To get an idea of the cost, consider these three quotes, provided by Churchill Insurance:

• A "gentleman farmer" aged 41, living in Devon, driving a Jaguar XJS 4-litre coupé worth £40,000. His premium will be £494 a year, provided he pays the first £200 of any claim (the compulsory excess). The same man driving a Ford Scorpio would pay £242 comprehensive, plus £200 voluntary excess.

• A 31-year-old Midlands male manager driving a Peugeot 406 will pay £263 a year, with no excess.

• A woman aged 27 living in West London driving a new Golf GTi would pay £655 with a £50 excess, or £603 with a £50 compulsory and £150 voluntary excess.

You can cut the premium substantially by agreeing to a higher excess fee, say £250. Be sure to ask your insurer about your no-claims discount and what circumstances will affect it. The standard no-claims discount for people under 50 is 65% of the premium — meaning that you get a discount of 65% on the premium, typically after three years of no claims.

But if you make a claim that year, the discount typically comes down to 55% when you next renew; and if you have two accidents, it may fall to as low as 30%.

There are ways of protecting your no-claims discount: for a flat fee most insurers will allow you to protect the hefty discount in the event of a claim on the policy. For £40, Churchill will preserve your discount even if you have two accidents in three years. You should also make sure that your policy offers

adequate back-up service.

Check, for example, whether your insurer guarantees a courtesy car if yours is out of action; check how long repairs are expected to take and whether they are guaranteed. You will not normally be given a courtesy car if yours is a write-off.

Car insurance is increasingly bought over the telephone from direct providers. These tend to offer better rates because they do not use brokers and have lower overheads. Direct Line is probably the best-known. The AA is also very competitive. But do ring around for at least three different quotes and terms.

There are many newcomers who use state-of-the-art technology to define your risk down to the smallest detail. They will use your full postcode so that your neighbours may actually be paying a different premium.

Q What are the main types of life assurance?

A They should really call it death assurance. When you buy a life policy, you are arranging for a sum of money to be paid out on your death. What could be simpler? Well, as you might expect, the insurance industry has managed to come up with a variety of contracts to suit a range of needs and circumstances.

The most straightforward type is "term" cover. This will pay out a chosen sum if you die during a specified period. If you survive beyond the term, the policy expires. You don't get any money back.

Whole-of-life policies pay out on your death, whenever it occurs. Term insurance may sound straightforward but there are several types on offer. "Renewable" cover means you can start again if you survive to the end of the original term without having to produce fresh evidence of good health. As a result, the premiums could be lower than if you were starting from scratch. However, premiums will still rise on account of your increased age.

With a "decreasing" term policy the sum paid falls over the period. This is used to match a debt which is gradually being repaid and means that you never have more cover than you need. When linked to a capital-and-interest (or repayment) mortgage, it is often called a mortgage-protection policy. Decreasing term cover is also used in inheritance tax planning.

Family-income benefit is a type of term cover that pays out an income instead of a lump sum. Typically, the policy will be arranged on the life of the family breadwinner over, say, a 20-year term. If that person dies after 12 years, the benefits are paid for the next eight years.

The cost of term insurance is determined by factors such

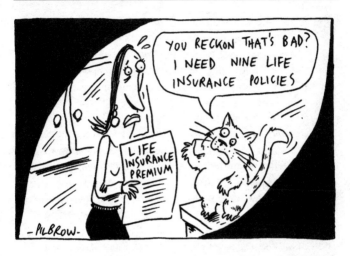

as your age, sex, health, whether you smoke, the length of the term and the size of the payout. Even though this is a basic sort of protection, it is worth looking around, or perhaps using an independent adviser, to trawl the market.

"Whole-of-life" insurance is more expensive than term cover because it pays out when you die, whenever that may be. You only pay premiums, however, until you are aged between 65 and 75.

Life insurance is also built into endowment policies, which are commonly used to repay an interest-only mortgage. The theory here is that the investment element of the endowment — available in "with-profits" and "unit-linked varieties" — will grow over the course of the mortgage to repay the debt when it falls due.

But if the borrower dies beforehand, the life insurance element of the contract clears the debt.

ⓠ Should I insure my income?

Ⓐ If you are used to a regular pay cheque, ask yourself how you would cope if your income suddenly dried up. If you fell ill or had an accident and could not work, where would the money come from to pay the mortgage? How would you run the car? What about new clothes? Or holidays?

If you think sick pay from your employer would tide you over, you could be seriously disappointed. The statutory minimum is £57.70 a week and your firm has to pay for only 28 weeks.

After this, you get short-term incapacity benefit of £57.70 a week — provided that you have paid enough National Insurance contributions.

If not, you go on means-tested income support, which means that if you have other sources of income — savings or a working partner — you might not get anything.

There are allowances for dependants, but even with a dependant adult and two children, benefits will barely top £100. If you are self-employed, you don't get statutory sick pay but go straight on to incapacity benefit — at a lower rate of £48.80. All benefits are taxable after six months. Long-term incapacity benefit begins after 53 weeks at £64.70 a week.

Eligibility is determined by your ability to do any work. If you are deemed fit but cannot find a job, you have to go on the dole.

All of which adds up to a convincing argument to insure your income. With an income-replacement policy, you get a monthly income until you are fit to work or until you reach retirement age. Since April 1996, benefits paid from such contracts are free of tax.

There are limits to the benefits, which means that when you combine your policy payout and any state benefits, you cannot get more than 75% of what you were earning. This is to stop malingerers staying at home because they are better off not working.

The cost of this sort of cover is determined by your age, sex, health and occupation. The amount of insurance you select will also affect the premium, as will the "deferred period" − the amount of time between your falling ill and the benefits being paid. You can choose anything from four weeks to two years. Providers include Norwich Union, Allied Dunbar and GAN.

Another way to counter the effects of losing your income is with mortgage-payment protection insurance (MPPI). This covers mortgage repayments and associated costs, such as home contents and buildings insurance. It differs from income-replacement insurance in that it also pays out if you are made redundant. It has become more popular since the government reduced the state help available.

If you took out your mortgage before October 1, 1995, you have to wait two months before you get any form of state assistance.

If you have taken out your mortgage since then, you could have to wait nine months before you receive assistance. And only the first £100,000 of your mortgage will be taken into account.

MPPI will pay your mortgage costs for up to 12 or 24 months or until you find another job or are fit enough to return to work. General Accident and SunAlliance are two of the biggest providers.

However, a word of warning: many income insurance policies are severely limited, and subject to strict terms and conditions hidden in the small print. So make sure you understand the policy.

Q How can I challenge my insurer over a claim?

A Insurance companies are notorious for saying no. They have even been known to have secret industry conferences to perfect various techniques for refusing claims. But if you have a genuine case, there are several ways of forcing their hand.

The first thing to bear in mind is that many insurers rely on your apathy. If they think they can get away with fobbing you off, they will. You must convince them that you will never let the matter rest.

Make sure you harangue the company and exhaust all its internal complaints procedures to get a final decision. Once it has made your blood boil with its indifference, the best bet is to go to the insurance ombudsman.

As soon as he has received your complaint, and you have had a letter of acknowledge-ment to that effect, write to the chief executive of the insurance company saying you are taking the matter to the ombudsman. That alone is often enough to force the

insurer to change its mind and make an immediate payout.

If it still refuses, the case should then go to adjudication. In 1997, the ombudsman ruled in favour of the policyholder in about one-third of the cases, which may not sound that impressive. But he argues that he is left with only the most tricky disputes because so many are settled as soon as the insurance company knows he is involved.

He has extensive powers to enforce big payouts — last year his largest award was for £203,125.

If the ombudsman rules in your favour, the insurance company has to pay out — no ifs or buts. But if he rules against you, you do not have to accept it. You are still free to take the matter to court.

The easiest way of doing this for claims less than £3,000 is through the small claims court. The process costs only about £70 and decisions are based on what the court calls "the balance of probabilities" – in other words, what common sense dictates. The court generally takes a sympathetic view, and it has a good record of ruling in the customer's favour.

The problem is that the companies can defend the case and often force it into a higher court, raising the prospect of huge legal expenses. Again, there are ways around this. Lloyd's offers an insurance policy called Greystoke Law-Assist.

It can be taken out at any point in the litigation to protect against the legal costs if you lose. Contact your nearest broker. In certain cases, where the details of the dispute fall outside the insurance ombudsman's terms of reference, he may not be allowed to adjudicate. If this happens, get a set of small claims court application forms, fill them in and send copies to the insurance company telling it you will post the papers to the court to book a hearing unless you receive a cheque within 28 days. This sometimes has the desired effect.

Another option is to contact the press. The prospect of bad publicity makes all insurers fearful. The Sunday Times has covered countless controversial insurance stories and is often successful in forcing a claim. One example involved a girl whose insurer refused to pay for her stolen clarinet until the story was reported.

Finally, you could follow the example of one infuriated customer who marched outside the insurer's offices wearing a sandwich board warning everybody to avoid its policies. However, the insurer still refused to pay his claim.

ℚ What sort of cover do I need to go abroad?

Ⓐ Holidays are all about buying summer clothes and novels to read on the beach or ski boots and thermal underwear. Overseas business trips are about negotiating contracts and cementing valuable relationships. They are not about insurance.

But if you fail to arrange the right sort of cover, your journey might turn into an expensive and uncomfortable experience. Most travel insurance is sold by travel agencies, which earn meaty commissions by getting you to sign up for cover when you pay for your holiday.

It used to be a nifty marketing ploy for travel firms to offer discounts on the package if you bought their policy. This conditional selling is almost always bad value, but the convenience of taking the cover offered by the agent remains persuasive.

Try and muster the effort to shop around. If you are a frequent international traveller who makes two trips a year or more you will probably be better off arranging an annual contract rather than cover for each journey.

It is worth asking about the extent of cover under an annual contract. Some will not insure you for winter

sports, for example, so if one of your trips is to the ski slopes, you may still be better served by dedicated policies.

If you are planning a long trip off the recognised tourist path, you will probably need specialist help. An insurance broker is always a good place to start, although a growing number of insurers offer deals direct to the public. Many banks and building societies also offer travel cover.

Top-of-the-range credit cardholders, for instance, often get free insurance, although with standard cards the protection may be limited.

Many household insurance policies are arranged on an

all-risks basis, which means possessions are insured outside the home.

Travel insurance covers medical expenses, liability, cancellation, curtailment, loss of baggage and theft. They will also pay out a lump sum if you are injured or if you die while abroad. The amount of insurance for each of these categories differs from contract to contract and you can normally save money by opting for lower levels of cover.

If you have an all-risks home contents policy, buy travel insurance that excludes cover for your possessions because these will already be covered.

Some policies offer a range of value-added services. For instance, if your car breaks down on the way to the airport or port, they will send a replacement to get you there on time, if possible, and contact the carrier to make alternative arrangements.

Drivers may need to make arrangements to cover their vehicles while abroad. Ask your existing motor insurer how much protection your policy provides and ask for a green card, which is proof in most European countries that you are insured.

Taxation

The Essential Questions:

ⓠ Who pays the most tax?

ⓐ You may not feel well-disposed towards the super-rich but when it comes to helping the economy, you have to take your hat off to them. The richest 1% of Britain's taxpayers pay a staggering 16% of the total income tax revenue, equal to almost £14 billion. The richest 5% pay more than a third of tax receipts, which is more than double what the poorest half contribute. They pay 13%, about £11 billion. Admittedly, the poorest feel the pinch more severely than the rich but if it were not for the mass of wealth they have created – or inherited – there would be much less money flowing into the government.

However, there are millions of pounds in overpaid tax sitting unclaimed at the Inland Revenue, waiting for the rightful owners to come forward. Most of these are thought to be lower earners who simply do not realise that they are being taxed wrongly on their savings because their income falls below the annual tax exemption.

Collectively, we paid a total of £210 billion in tax during the 1997-98 tax year. That was divided between 10.6m single people, 9.2m husbands and 6m wives. Of total tax paid, about £116 billion was income tax, £89.2 billion was

VAT and £4.4 billion was car tax. The figures have changed radically since the last Labour government, when the richest 5% paid about 25% of the income tax total. That suggests the Tories were more severe in taxing the rich, but this is not the case. It is simply that the rich have got much richer in the past 17 years.

Average earnings for Britain's richest 10% have almost doubled in real terms, from £300 a week to more than £500 a week, while the poorest 10% have seen wages hardly move from their 1979 level of £60 a week. The

poorest taxpayers may not have much to sing about but the 1980s boom has helped almost 2m more workers break into the higher rate tax band of 40%, payable on earnings over £27,100 from April 1998. In the 1970s there were only about 600,000 higher rate taxpayers. Part of that rise may be due to the attitude of the rich to taxation. In the 1970s, when tax on investment income was 98% and the higher rate on ordinary earnings was a ridiculous 87%, nobody wanted to pay anything.

If you qualified for tax at that rate you could afford a good accountant, and the amount they paid was nominal. Since the higher rate has dropped to a more realistic level, fewer people seek to evade the tax.

Q What is tax-deductible?

A There are several ways to reduce the amount of income tax you pay. In some instances, deductions are made out of gross income; in others, you can secure an adjustment to your tax code that leaves you with more of your income intact – if you get married, for example.

In addition, everybody has certain tax allowances. These are the sums deducted from your income before it is taxed. The personal allowance for somebody under 65 is £4,195 from April 1998, which means that if your income is below this level, you pay no tax.

Higher allowances are available to those aged 65 to 74 (£5,410) and from 75 and over (£5,600) from April 1997. Additional personal allowances are available to those bringing up children on their own, the blind and to widows. Remember also that there are three income-tax bands. The first £4,300 of taxable income is taxed at 20%, the next £22,800 at 23% and any income over £27,100 at 40%.

Tax-planning strategies are often designed to "reduce" income so that it falls in a lower band. For example, when half of a married couple has a high income (perhaps from a portfolio of investments) and the other very little, assets can be transferred to make full use of each individual's allowances.

Pension contributions receive relief at your highest rate, which means that for a higher rate taxpayer, a £1,000 premium in effect costs £600. Somebody paying basic rate tax can secure £1,000 of pension benefits for £770.

The taxman's generosity is not limitless. Employees can save up to only 15% of their salary in a company pension while those with a personal pension can invest from 17.5% to 40%, depending on

Taxation

their age, to a maximum of £87,600 as from April 1998.

Tax relief is available to mortgage borrowers through the Miras system, which now provides 10% relief on the interest payable on loans up to £30,000, provided the loan is used to buy or improve your own home, reduced from 15% in April 1998.

Basic rate tax relief is no longer available on medical insurance premiums paid by or on behalf of a person over 60 – the relief was axed in the 1998 budget.

Maintenance payments to a former spouse also count as deductions. The recipient is exempt from the tax on the amount while the payer gets relief up to a maximum of £1,900 from April 1998. However, this relief is limited to just 15% of the total allowance.

Money can be given tax efficiently to a charity, either through a deed of covenant or a payroll-giving scheme or Gift Aid. Labour introduced a new tax-efficient way of giving to Third World countries in 1998.

Certain job expenses can also be used to reduce the income tax bill. Your tax inspector will be able to explain what this means in practice. The self-employed, particularly those working from home, should also discuss what can be deducted from the gross income to cut the tax bill.

In addition, taxpayers can receive up to £4,250 per annum tax-free in rent from letting furnished accommodation in their home.

Investments in enterprise schemes and venture capital trusts offer generous income tax relief (as well as capital gains tax deferral). These are risky products and should be considered after secure tax-efficient vehicles such as pensions, personal equity plans and Tessas (and, from April 1999, ISAs).

ⓆHow can I reduce my inheritance tax?

Ⓐ Inheritance tax (IHT) is seen by some as the cruellest tax of them all. After a lifetime of working, saving and paying the mortgage, 40% of everything you have worked so hard to accumulate, above the first £223,000 (raised by £8,000 in the 1998 budget), goes straight back to the Inland Revenue.

Fortunately, the legislation is so riddled with loopholes that, with a bit of planning, few people need pay anything at all. Indeed, the former politician Roy Jenkins once famously described the tax as "a voluntary levy paid by those who distrust their heirs more than they dislike the Inland Revenue".

It was feared Labour would take a harsh view of IHT and close most of the loopholes. So it was surprising that Gordon Brown in his 1998 budget lifted the tax-free threshold by £8,000, and left the loopholes untouched. Of course, this leniency may change in future budgets.

There are six basic exemptions that can be used to reduce your estate to beneath the threshold. First, married couples need not worry. Transfers of wealth between spouses are completely free of tax. The same does not apply to unmarried couples, however. If one dies, leaving the estate to the survivor, there could be a hefty tax bill.

Then you can make tax-free "gifts" from your capital of up to £3,000 each year.

If your income can stand it, you can take advantage of the "normal expenditure" exemption. This allows tax-free gifts from income, but with a catch. Although there is no stated limit, the gifts cannot be so large as to lower the giver's usual standard of living and it must be a regular payment.

Other exemptions include the small gifts exemption, which allows a further £250 a year to be given tax-free to as

many individuals as you like; and the marriage gifts exemption, allowing £5,000 to be given to a child, £2,500 to a grandchild or £1,000 to anyone else who is getting married.

The most valuable way of reducing IHT liability is the "potentially exempt transfer". This allows gifts of any size to be made at any time, but they escape the tax only if the giver survives for seven years after making the gift.

In addition, the giver cannot continue to benefit from the gift in any way, so if you give the house to your children, you must either move out immediately or pay an open-market rent. Similarly, if you give a painting, it must be removed and hung in the recipient's house immediately.

Trust law also offers ways around IHT, but these are expensive and complex to set up. You should see a solicitor specialising in trust law.

Q How do I avoid capital gains tax?

A One of the biggest changes announced in the 1998 budget was to the way capital gains are taxed.

Previously any gain over the tax-free allowance (£6,800 from April 1998) was taxed at your marginal rate, after allowing for the effects of inflation.

But from April 1998 a new system took effect known as "tapered relief". Essentially, this means you are taxed less the longer you hold on to your shares.

The new CGT rates start at 40% or 23%, depending on your rate band, and gradually fall over 10 years to a minimum of 24% for higher rate tax payers and 13.8% for basic rate tax payers.

If you hold them for just a year, for example, you are taxed at the highest rate. If you hold your assets for five years, you will be taxed at 34% or 19.5%. The idea is to encourage people to hold on to their investments for a longer period, thus boosting investment in British industry.

There were two further, fundamental changes to CGT in the 1998 budget. Indexation, by which you were previously allowed to deduct

from any liability the gains attributable to inflation, was removed altogether to simplify the calculation of CGT.

This is all very well in a low inflationary environment, but if inflation should return, many people will be worse off, regardless of the tapered reliefs. In this respect, the Chancellor's abolition of indexation relief may backfire.

The Chancellor, Gordon Brown, also abolished "bed and breakfasting", one of the most popular forms of legal tax avoidance. It meant that you could sell your shares one day and buy them back the next, thus realising the gain and using up your tax allowance with minimal risk.

In this way, investors were able to establish a higher base price for their shares without paying any immediate tax.

Now, any sales and subsequent purchases within a 30-day period will be treated as though the gain (or loss) had never been realised. The problem with waiting 30 days to buy back your shares is that the price may well have increased, and any tax saved may be offset by the cost of repurchasing the shares.

Accountants and tax experts have already started to find ways around the removal of bed and breakfasting.

One such is "bed and pepping". This is where you sell your shares and use your annual CGT allowance, then buy them back the next day through a personal equity plan (Pep).

Profits made within a Pep are free of all tax (the same will apply to individual savings accounts when they arrive in April 1999). There are, of course, limits to how much you can put into a Pep or ISA.

Another suggestion is "bed and spousing", where one married partner sells the family's shares and the other buys them back the next day, thus stripping out the CGT liability while keeping the shares within the family. Transfers of assets between spouses are deemed not to have yielded either a profit or loss for CGT purposes, so once the 30 days have elapsed, the shares may be transferred back to the original holder.

There are more complicated methods, using futures and options to hedge against a rise or fall in the shares during the 30-day period, but these are not recommended to small investors.

Indeed, most people pay no CGT because their gains, if any, often fall within their £6,800 allowance.

Q How do I reclaim overpaid tax?

A There are few easy ways to make money these days but here is one of them. Get in touch with the Inland Revenue and reclaim all the tax you have overpaid.

A recent report suggested there was more than £5.5 billion overpaid each year, but this is a notional figure because much of this is "overpaid" as a result of neglecting tax-efficient savings vehicles such as Tessas and Peps. This is not overpaying in the true sense because it is not reclaimable unless you are a non-taxpayer who can reclaim any tax that has been wrongly deducted by your bank or building society.

However, there is about £500m in real cash sitting in the Revenue's coffers, waiting for the 6m rightful owners to come forward.

The tax is often overpaid by people not making full use of their allowances – single people getting married and not telling the Revenue, for example.

However, the biggest single cause is non-taxpayers forgetting to tell their building society, so income tax is still deducted on all interest they earn. This group, totalling about 4.5m, mostly consists of pensioners, expatriates, students and those on low incomes. If you fall into this group the interest on your savings will automatically be taxed at 20% unless you take the appropriate steps.

If you think you may be entitled to a rebate, or even if you haven't a clue, why not try for one? For the time it takes to fill in a form you could get a cheque for hundreds.

The first thing is to get a copy of the imaginatively named leaflet IR110. This explains the procedure and also contains form R40, which you must fill in. Send it off to the Inland Revenue. You should hear within 28 days whether you are eligible.

The system has been improved from the days when claims were rerouted around various regional tax offices; they are now handled more centrally, which means fewer chances of mistakes and the likelihood of a quick response.

If you need to have your interest credited gross to your savings accounts, fill in form R85. They are all available from post offices.

Often there is confusion because the Revenue has made a mistake. This is by no means rare because it is estimated that about £200m is overpaid each year as a result of Revenue errors. The chances of Revenue error have increased with the shift to self-assessment in 1998. Thousands claim to have been wrongly penalised for supposed late payment of tax.

In self-assessment cases, you are free to appeal against the penalty. Other cases may require a meeting with the local inspector. Usually, this is enough to resolve the dispute but if you are still not satisfied you will have to go to the Inland Revenue Adjudicator, Elizabeth Filkin.

Filkin has the power to look at all aspects of the Revenue's dealings, whether it be erroneous tax bills, delays in getting refunds or simply rudeness by staff. She can award compensation or insist the Revenue pays out on a claim, but she cannot make decisions about tax law. If you think the Revenue is wrong because it is misinterpreting the law, you will be directed to the Special Commissioners, employed by the Lord Chancellor's department. They will clarify any disagreements.

The adjudicator has been known to force payouts for administrative errors and prevented the Revenue from collecting tax that was underpaid as a result of its own inefficiencies.

Q What happens if I evade tax?

A At worst, you will go to jail; at best, you may escape with only a small fine – plus interest on your unpaid tax bill. It all depends on whether the Inland Revenue believes you wilfully or accidentally evaded tax, and to what extent. Ignorance is no defence in tax matters, so all tax evaders should expect punishment.

Tax evasion comes in many guises. Usually it involves understating the amount of tax payable by exaggerating or manipulating deductions, putting assets out of reach of the tax man – in an offshore account, for example – or full-scale fraud.

How do they catch you? The Revenue is very different from the sluggish animal of a decade ago. These days, it is a lean, mean, hi-tech machine able to swoop on the tiniest taxpayer at the press of a button. Gordon Brown, the Chancellor, announced in the 1998 budget a crackdown on tax dodgers through a new "anti-avoidance" law, a catch-all ruling that could shut many loopholes and make legal avoidance evasion in the eyes of the Revenue.

More terrifying, tax collectors are paid bonuses for the amount of tax they collect. If they suspect you of tax dodging, they will initiate an investigation. And, from 1998 they can launch an investigation into your tax affairs without warning under "random audit" rules introduced on 5 April 1997, when the new self-assessment regime came into effect.

The Revenue says it will always give you the chance to explain any apparent omission from your accounts or returns.

Accountants recommend you say nothing to the Revenue until absolutely necessary. It is worth taking their advice.

The Revenue can insist on a meeting (you do not have to attend, but it is thought

advisable) and has the power to obtain any documents such as business records and bank statements.

If caught evading tax, the penalty will normally be a percentage of tax underpaid or paid late. The Revenue's penalties start at 100% of unpaid tax but come down depending on how much you disclose, whether you co-operate and the gravity of the offence.

You may get a 30% cut in the penalty for voluntary disclosure and 40% for full co-operation. If the offence is minor, a 40% reduction in the penalty may be granted.

For example, say the inspector has granted a 15% reduction for disclosure, 30% for co-operation and 20% for gravity, giving a total of 65%. The penalty will therefore be 35% of unpaid tax.

But if you provide no information, refuse to attend meetings or plain lie, the tax inspector will throw the book at you.

You may make an offer, which, if accepted, amounts to a contract. If you are unhappy with the way your case is handled, contact the Revenue controller for your area, the adjudicator or the tax ombudsman.

Remember, you can ask the Revenue to explain its actions and your rights at any time during the investigation.

Under new penalties introduced with self-assessment, late tax will incur an instant £100 penalty plus interest, and subsequent penalties for further delays. The annual deadline for self-assessed tax is 31 January.

Q How does self-assessment work?

A Self-assessment affects the 9m or so taxpayers who already receive intimidating tax returns every April. These include higher rate payers, the self-employed, company partners and those with complicated tax affairs. However, it does not mean you have to work out all your tax liabilities yourself, although you can if you wish. Whatever way you do it, you will have to keep thorough records of your earnings and expenditure. Under the new system, which began in April 1997, taxpayers have to complete a new-style return using actual figures, stating their precise income, including earnings from investments, property, business activities and employers.

It will no longer be acceptable to say "as per accounts" or "as per employer" as it used to be.

The figures must relate to income earned in the previous 12 months. That means keeping thorough records of earnings — interest on building society accounts, dividend payments from shares, even mileage in a company car.

You will also have the choice of whether to calculate the tax liability yourself, based on your income minus your allowances, or let the Inland Revenue do it for you.

If the Inland Revenue does it, it will calculate your liability according to your figures. It says it trusts the taxpaying public but will be making vigorous random checks to make sure everybody is telling the truth.

If you opt to have the Revenue work out your liability, you must send back the completed return by 30 September, in each tax year. If you do the sums yourself, you have until 31 January in each tax year to file them. By that date you must also pay the first half of any estimated tax due for the current tax year; the second

deadlines are non-negotiable and anybody who does not meet them will face an immediate penalty.

If you do not file your return on time, you will receive a £100 penalty, even if it is just one day late. If it is still not received six months later, you will be fined another £100. If you are late with your actual tax payment, you will have to pay interest on the outstanding amount, as is the case today. If you are more than 28 days late, you will pay a penalty equivalent to 5% of the outstanding tax bill. The Revenue also classes erroneous or incomplete returns as late. You could even be fined as much as £60 a day (in penalties) for very late unpaid tax, plus interest. So be warned.

half is payable by 31 July. For example, by 31 January 1998, you will have had to pay any outstanding tax for 1996-97 plus half your estimated liability (if any) for 1997-98, and the rest by 31 July. But what if the estimates are wrong? Then, an adjustment is made at the end of the year. Say, for example, you paid half your 97-98 liability of £10,000 on 31 January, 1998 and the other half in July, and it later transpires your actual liability was £15,000. Then you will have to pay the balance of £5,000 by 31 January, 1999. These

Q How can I challenge my council tax bill?

A The council tax has been branded as one the most unfair and inconsistent of all taxes, with the exception of its predecessor, the poll tax. Millions of people may be paying too much because of a ludicrous valuation system that is outdated and hopelessly inaccurate. The tax is calculated according to the value of the property and then split into bands from A to H. In England, the bandings are standard across the country, but in Scotland and Wales they can vary.

In England, houses up to £40,000 are in Band A; up to £52,000 in Band B; up to £68,000 in Band C; up to £88,000 in Band D; up to £120,000 in Band E; up to £160,000 in Band F; up to £320,000 in Band G and more than £320,000 in Band H.

The values were set by a nationwide valuation programme carried out in 1991. At best, it was haphazard. The National Audit Office conservatively estimates that 2m properties were inaccurately valued at that time. Even so, these valuations still apply. The government gave residents leave to challenge their valuation between April and November 1993 and about 1m appealed. But that still leaves at least 1m people paying too much tax who may no longer complain.

Taxpayers can challenge their banding only in a limited number of circumstances. A resident can propose a change if there has been a "material reduction" in the property's value — say, if a garage or extension has been demolished.

Taxpayers also have leave to appeal if the "physical state of the dwellings' locality has changed" — in other words, if a motorway now cuts through your back garden or a sewage plant has been built nearby. It is also possible to appeal if you are a new taxpayer,

provided an appeal has not already been considered and it is lodged within six months. But again, you can only question the 1991 valuation. The argument that you bought your home for less than the valuation price does not count with the Revenue. Annoyingly, you cannot appeal if the value of your home has fallen.

To appeal against your council tax banding, first contact your local authority, which will put you in touch with the Valuation Office Agency, the division of the Revenue that deals with appeals. Collect as much evidence as possible to back your claim. If the valuation officer accepts your case, the listing will be altered. If not, you could end up at an appeals tribunal. You can, however, reduce your council tax bill if you are separated or divorced from your spouse, and live apart.

❓ How does the tax system support families?

🅐 The 1998 budget substantially eased the tax system in favour of lower-earning parents who want to work but find the cost of childcare makes the effort pointless. For that, many families will be grateful.

The new childcare tax credit, to be introduced from April 2000, will enable parents to claim up to £100 a week for registered childcare if they have one child under 11, and up to £150 if they have two or more children.

The benefits will be restricted, however, to parents who earn up to £30,000 a year.

Until now, many parents decided not to seek work because the high cost of childcare absorbs most of their earnings.

The government's tax change will mean that women like Jenny, of South London, may reconsider job offers which she previoulsy turned down.

As a single mother, Jenny receives income support of £64.07 a week and £17 for lone parent and child benefit. Her council tax and rent are paid by the Department of Social Security.

Nursery costs of £66 for three days would have wiped out her earnings from the job, which paid £5.25 an hour. The Family Credit Hotline calculated that she would be just £14 a week better off.

Jenny argues that there was no point in putting herself and son through all the upheaval for such a small difference in income. The nursery also requested a registration fee and two weeks' deposit, which she could not afford.

The childcare tax credit aims to change all that. The credit will form part of a new Working Families Tax Credit (WFTC) which is to replace the current family credit system due to be phased out in October 1998. As a result, it is estimated 400,000 families will be added to the 800,000 that currently benefit from family credit.

Parents who work more than 16 hours a week will be eligible for the new childcare tax credit. The amount they receive will depend on the number of children in the family under 11, total family income and whether this is derived from full- or part-time work. Anyone earning £30,000 or less who has two children under 11 will receive some credit; the maximum credit will go to those on £17,000 a year or less with two children under 11.

The credit will be in addition to any existing benefits received – the present system gives 30,000 families help with childcare costs.

Jenny's position is therefore greatly improved. Under WFTC, low-paid families will receive an extra £48.80 a week in basic tax credit, plus £14.85 per week for each child under the age of 11, £20.45 for a child between 11 and 16, and £25.40 for those aged 16 to 18. Parents will also receive an extra £10.80 a week if they work more than 30 hours. The ultimate aim is to ensure that every parent in full-time work receives a minimum wage of £180 a week.

According to the DSS, if Jenny went out to work part-time and earned £90 a week, the new WFTC would almost double her income – £48.80 in basic credit, £14.85 for her child, and £17.10 in existing single parent and child benefit, an income of £168.15 a week.

The problem is, for many parents such as Jenny, the changes will come in to effect too late for them to take advantage.

Married couples, however, did not fare any better after the 1998 budget, when their tax allowance was cut slightly.

Q Should I become a tax exile?

A Becoming a tax exile is not an end in itself. Do so only if you really want an overseas job or have large amounts of money — enough to justify the costs of living abroad. A life spent escaping tax can be a lonely, unsettling one. Images come to mind of gin-soaked, cowboy-booted blondes prancing about the bars of Marbella; or perennially suntanned loafers roaming the world in search of the perfect ski resort.
A more accurate image is the celebrity or businessman who has a house in several countries but is a permanent resident of none.

He or she is often a "resident" of an offshore financial centre such as the Channel Islands, Monaco, the Bahamas or Luxembourg. Such people, often described as "super-rich", inhabit the realm of so-called "international people" for whom nowhere is "home". Their lives prove the point of Leona Helmsley, wife of a wealthy property developer, that "only the little people pay tax".

The truth is, most tax exiles are more ordinary folk, drawn overseas by a high-paid job on a Middle East oil field or the chance to retire in the Spanish sun.

Freed from the Inland Revenue's prying eyes, their first priority is to establish an "offshore" bank account in a tax haven into which their salaries or retirement income is paid. Offshore bank accounts are completely tax-free for non-residents, and all the leading banks and building societies offer them from their subsidiaries in places such as the Channel Islands, the Isle of Man and Gibraltar.

Another kind of tax exile is the moderately wealthy with overseas assets who like their home country but who hate being taxed on their world-wide income (as British tax laws do). So they choose to spend half the year abroad and half the year at home, thus achieving the coveted status of a "non-resident" in the UK for tax purposes.

This can be trickier than you think. To be regarded as a UK resident by the Inland Revenue you must be physically present in the country for six months or more in any one tax year.

So, to be regarded as non-resident, you must spend less than that period living in Britain in a tax year. There are no exceptions, says the Revenue.

The deadline makes for some intriguing annual itineraries in tax exiles' lives: last-minute scrambles for the airport to escape the "tax axe" are not unknown.

One reason people have always become tax exiles is to retire abroad, drawing on their offshore savings tax-free. However, Labour promised to crack down on that practice in the 1998 budget, pledging to introduce legislation to prohibit overseas assets escaping tax.

Many people use the United Kingdom as a tax haven and are deemed to be "tax exiles" by their country of origin: many Scandinavians fall into this category. They are resident in the UK but domiciled abroad, a status that gives them the right to avoid paying tax on their worldwide assets.

Wealthy Arabs and Americans, and other rich foreigners resident in the UK enjoy non-domiciled status. As a result, they pay tax only on their overseas income stream while avoiding tax completely on their offshore capital. In return they provide racehorses, beautiful works of art and a great many jobs.

Labour has threatened to close that loophole.

Planning for retirement

The Essential Questions:

Q Will the state support me in my retirement?

A The short answer is no. The long answer is only if you have made no pension provision of your own, and qualify fully for DSS (Department of Social Security) benefit. Then you can expect to receive state income support plus the basic state pension of £61 a week for a single person or about £90 for a married couple.

The basic pension is available automatically to all. But it is barely enough to live on. Many people will also require income support, set according to your needs. But to receive income support you have to pass a means test; in other words, you have to prove you are poor. Pride inhibits many people who have worked all their lives, or raised children, from applying for income support when they retire. So they live in penury. Indeed, the DSS accepts that 1m more people could claim retirement benefit than actually do. But already about a third of retired people rely on the state for their income.

That will have to change, because Labour says it will

not be able to foot the bill in future. And if the government cannot support you, who will? The answer is glaringly obvious to anyone who realises the seriousness of the problem: only yourself, and perhaps your family.

Even if you think state support is ample for your needs, don't expect it to stay that way: the basic pension is being slowly whittled down. One reason is that the previous government decided in the early 1980s that it should rise in line with inflation, not wages. But wages tend to outstrip inflation, so the effect is slowly to erode the buying power of the basic pension.

Both the Conservatives and Labour have shown interest in

all-purpose, tax-free savings accounts that would serve as "second-tier" pensions to the state system. Some MPs are in favour of compulsory contributions to a level that would ensure we all retire in reasonable comfort and Labour's leaders have signalled that they may commit to compulsory second-tier schemes . . . but not yet.

We all may have to some day: the cost of retirement is frightening. To retire in any sort of comfort, you must start contributing to a pension scheme as early as possible. Consider this: to achieve an annual income in retirement of £10,000, a 35-year-old with no pension provision would have to pay £208 a month into a pension fund. To retire at 60, the figure is £283 and for those who hope to stop working early, at 55, a whacking £397.

For a 25-year-old, the respective contribution levels are £145, £186 and £245; but they rise to £335, £507 and £848 a month for a 45-year-old. People in their 50s who have made no pension provision face far higher payments, and will probably have to rely on the state to support them. But these contributions will only buy £10,000 a year. Most people would like more than that. To enjoy the same standard of living in retirement as you did during employment, you will need to contribute at least 15% of your gross income to a pension fund.

The self-employed in particular should consider some form of pension provision because they are more likely to let their savings lapse.

It is clear that many people will have to change their lifestyles in order to fund their retirement – eg, by buying an old banger instead of spending £300 per month on a new car.

Q Is a traditional pension still the best option?

A Since the personal equity plan appeared on the scene in 1986, this question has been the subject of fierce debate. Some argue that Peps can be more effective tools for retirement planning because of their flexibility and the way their tax status allows their proceeds to be taken tax-free. However, for most people, the pension – be it a personal or company pension – remains the most suitable method.

Peps and pensions are similar savings schemes. They both invest in stocks and shares to make money grow as rapidly as possible, and both are given a favourable tax status.

However, the situation is now markedly different with the introduction of individual savings accounts (ISAs) in April 1999. These only allow contributions of £5,000 a year, whereas you could put £9,000 a year into Peps (double both figures for married couples). So ISAs will be far less suitable as long term savings plans for retirement because their size is so restricted. Nonetheless, they will serve as good "second-tier" pensions for most people. Just how good, depends on how much you put in and how your underlying assets perform. Whatever happens, ISAs' tax situation is much the same as Peps.

With Peps, the money you contribute will already have been subject to income tax. The contributions will grow within the Pep, and any withdrawals can be taken totally tax-free.

With pensions, your contributions are tax-free because they are subject to tax relief at your highest rate. This means that the government will refund the income tax straight into your pension fund.

Consequently, a basic rate taxpayer need only contribute £77 to put £100 into his or

I'D LIKE MY PENSION NOW AND TO START WORK WHEN I'M 65

a Pep who contributed £6,000 would have £21,850 after 15 years, assuming the same growth rate (and less, with an ISA). Pep/ISA income is, of course, tax-free, but the holder must decide whether

her pension.

This tax relief means that, for the same contributions, pensions savers are actually contributing more than those with a Pep (or ISA). Even taking into account the fact that the pension proceeds are taxable, this still works out better in most cases. For example, £6,000 paid by a higher rate taxpayer into a pension would be £10,000 after tax relief, and after 15 years, the fund would have grown to £35,500, assuming growth at 9%. Somebody with

an annuity until death offers a better deal, albeit taxable.

Using our examples, the pension holder (personal or company money purchase) could buy an annuity paying about £3,550 a year, which is subject to tax, while the Pep holder, after buying a life annuity, could expect £2,885 a year, which is also part taxable.

For most people, the best bet seems to be the pension, although Peps/ISAs are far more flexible and certainly a recommended supplement.

ⓠ Should I join my company pension scheme?

ⓐ Yes. There are hardly any circumstances in which you would be better off elsewhere – say in a personal pension. This will be unpleasant news to thousands who were persuaded in the pensions mis-selling fiasco of the late 1980s to opt out of their company schemes and set up personal pensions. Those who did so are understandably angry with insurers and financial advisers who failed to warn them of the risks.

Compare the monthly contribution in a company scheme to a personal pension, where you may put in 5% of your salary. Obviously, your final retirement fund will be smaller because your employer will probably not be contributing to it.

Group personal pensions may be a good halfway house because employers usually contribute to them. They are preferable to a single personal pension taken out in your own name because of their flexibility and benefits.

A small minority of company pension schemes offer poor value; for example, where the employer contributes a small percentage of basic salary, such as 2% or 3%, or where

the fund performs badly. But these are rare.

There may be cases where you decide to opt out because you want to reinvest your pension contribution into your own personal pension. People who move jobs regularly or who want to retain more of their take-home pay may fall into these categories.

Many people wish to supplement their pension contributions with additional voluntary contributions (AVCs). These are an excellent way of building up an even larger retirement fund, but you may consider investing in a personal equity plan instead.

AVCs, like pension

contributions, attract tax relief on the premiums but the final benefits are taxed as income; with Peps, there is no up-front tax relief but the income is tax-free. A general rule is that AVCs are better for basic rate taxpayers and Peps better for higher rate taxpayers, because Peps allow income to be taken tax-free.

Company pensions are not infallible, however: their income was effectively slashed in the 1997 budget by 10–20% due to the removal of tax relief on dividends (applied to personal pensions, too). The Pensions Act, which was introduced in April 1997, means company pension schemes are now properly regulated. And a compensation scheme is in place for those who lose their pension through fraud.

Q How do I choose a personal pension?

A Assuming you cannot join an occupational pension scheme, you will have to take out a personal pension. Everybody has heard of the big pension providers: Prudential, Allied Dunbar, Legal & General and so on. But asking for their literature and assessing which pension is right for you is a tricky business, and leaves most people with glazed eyes after just a few minutes' consideration.

After the pensions mis-selling scandal, where hundreds of thousands of people were sold inappropriate pension plans, public faith in insurers and their salesmen has plummeted, making that route seem risky too.

However, with preparation, you can ensure you get the best deal. If you are collared by a salesman, be prepared to blitz him or her with questions. Salesmen are driven by commission and some can by very persuasive but it is important not to be intimidated.

First, find out about a provider's financial strength. This is particularly relevant for pensions because they are such long-term investments.

How flexible is the pension? Can you reduce, increase, stop or restart payments without penalty? If your circumstances change, this flexibility will be vital.

Can you convert it into a freestanding additional voluntary contributions (AVC) plan if you later qualify for an occupational scheme? If you cannot, the provider may penalise you for stopping the contributions, and then you could be hit for more charges as you establish a separate freestanding AVC scheme.

Also ask if you can retire early without penalty. Many companies impose hefty charges if you dare to retire before 65.

How high are the charges?

And, importantly, how good is the company's historic investment performance? This is no guarantee of future returns, but a company that is a consistently bad performer is probably best avoided.

These are all essential questions, but even after getting all the answers, you should seek out a second opinion. Most of the answers will not make much sense unless you get an expert to explain how that particular pension stacks up against others in the market.

You can check these questions through an independent financial adviser (IFA) — you may prefer one who charges a fee, rather than commission — who will be able to compare the pension with all its competitors, and possibly suggest a better alternative.

However, IFAs have not emerged unscathed from the pensions mis-selling scandal, and you will have to quiz them on their credentials too.

Just because they are classified as independent does not mean they cannot be swayed by hefty commissions.

Amanda Davidson, a partner of IFA Holden Meehan, suggests clients ask exacting questions of their adviser, and her firm produces a list of essential questions which people can ask. These include whether or not the adviser is truly independent. Does he work on commission or on a fee basis? If the IFA works on a commission basis, demand at least two recommendations. How long has the IFA been in business? Is the IFA qualified and who is he regulated by? What are the IFA's areas of expertise? If an adviser specialises in mortgages, finding one that concentrates on pensions probably makes more sense.

Also, ask how many clients the IFA has, and what other services you can expect. Even after all this, it may still make sense to get a second opinion.

Q How do I get the best annuity deal?

A Use an annuity broker. You may not be aware of the better deals available to those with a shorter life expectancy, with illnesses, or who smoke or drink excessively. People in these categories can expect a far better annuity rate than healthy people — as much as 5%-10% more. This is because of the macabre truth that they may die earlier, so they get a better payout from their pension fund.

Women traditionally get lower annuity rates than men because, on average, they live longer. Remember, an annuity is simply an annual income paid out of your pension fund until you die. So the lower your life expectancy, the higher your income because the distribution of your life savings is compressed into a shorter period.

Annuity rates have plunged in the past five years, along with interest rates, from about 16% to 11%. Pensioners are worse off, but their loss is offset by their pension funds, which will have risen because stock markets have performed very well in the past two years.

But just because inflation is low does not mean it will stay that way. It is a good idea to protect your annuity against the ravages of rising inflation. This is the most important piece of financial advice for anyone retiring now into Britain's low inflation environment, but it is little heeded.

The reason to protect your annuity is simple: inflation is at a 30-year low of 2.8%, yet the average inflation rate over the past 30 years is 8.27%. Inflation may well rise in coming years.

So if you buy a fixed, or "level" annuity — as 80% of retiring people do — which pays a fixed annual income for life, you will see your purchasing power gradually erode as inflation rises.

Experts recommend that you protect yourself against inflation by choosing an annuity that will escalate in line with the Retail Price Index. One option might be to buy an annuity that rises at a fixed percentage, say up to 8.5% a year, subject to Inland Revenue restrictions.

The problem with rising, or "escalating", annuities is that your starting income will be considerably lower because the total payout is greater than with fixed annuities.

However, remember that on average you are likely to live longer, so your eventual savings may well offset the early shortfall. Insurers are adjusting their annuity rates to take account of longer life expectancy.

Look at it this way: you would not take a job if you knew you were going to get the same salary for 20 years.

Yet most men and women retire for 13 and 17 years respectively on the same income. You may also want to consider one of the new pension draw-down plans, where you take your tax-free lump sum in one go and write a cheque to yourself each year, or month, out of that sum — as long as the income stays within the limits set by the government actuary.

You would invest the remaining 75% in investments of your choice, drawing down income from these investments provided they perform sufficiently to maintain it. You must be sure not to pay yourself more than the interest built up or you will eat into your capital. You must, however, buy an annuity from age 75.

Another option is a phased retirement plan, where you slice off a bit of your lump sum gradually. In these, your tax-free cash comes through gradually.

Q What if I'm sold a duff pension?

A If you have a personal pension, the chances are it was wrongly sold to you. During the course of the investigation into the pensions mis-selling scandal, in which well over 2m people have been wrongly sold personal pensions since their inception in 1988, it has emerged that as many as 90% of all policies were taken out as the result of bad advice.

The problem is that most people do not know when they are mis-sold a pension. It is not like being burgled – there is no immediate shock. That would come years later, on retirement, when your lifelong workmate told you how much larger his pension was because he had stayed in his occupational scheme. And all those years before, you were persuaded to buy a personal pension instead.

The government is now embarking on a new initiative to alert people to the fact they may have been mis-sold as part of the second phase of its pension review.

The first phase, which deals with the 580,000 or so "priority cases", mostly those already retired, approaching retirement or dead, is on the way to completion and should be finished altogether by the end of this year. The second phase focuses on the 1.8m or so "non-priority" victims.

If you are not involved in the compensation process, then it is worth finding out whether or not you should be.

Basically, if you were in , or had access to, an occupational pension when you were sold a personal pension, then you are probably in line for some compensation.

Get in touch with the insurance company or Independent Financial Adviser that sold you your policy and ask for your case to be reviewed. Ideally, if you have access to a company scheme, you should join it and have your personal

NO HEART, NO BRAINS, NO COURAGE, NO SCRUPLES

PENSION SALESMAN

-PILBROW-

pension contributions, plus compensation to make up for missed employer contributions and investment growth paid in too. If you are not satisfied with the response from whoever sold you your policy, contact the PIA for further advice. It has a Pension Helpline on 0171-417-7001, or you could contact the FSA public enquiries office on 0845-606-1234.

If you do not have access to a company scheme, and want to take out a personal pension, then make sure you ask plenty of questions to ensure you are sold the right policy. Commission charges vary according to what type you take. Ask how charges compare between single premium and regular premium policies. Usually, the commission will be much less for a lump sum than for regular premium policies. Also find out about the penalties imposed if you miss a month's premiums — many people want to take premium holidays if they fall on hard times.

Ask whether it would be better paying, say, £100 a month plus the occasional £200 single premium rather than a regular £200 premium. Many people overstretch themselves and may be penalised as a result.

Be sure to ask about premium waiver benefits. If you are unable to work through illness or accident, the insurer will continue paying your contributions.

❓ What happens to my pension if I get divorced?

🅐 Until now, a husband has tended to keep his pension when negotiating a divorce; the wife has usually taken the family home (along with the children).

Family lawyers say this has always been the typical settlement. They know they can challenge the husband over his pension, but rarely do. So although a non-earning divorced woman may have somewhere to live, she often has no income in old age apart from maintenance and state support.

That is all changing. Since 1 July 1996, wives who divorce have been able to earmark their husband's pension so that when he retires, a proportion of his retirement fund is payable to them.

This new law has received cross-party support, and was deemed fair by both left and right-wing MPs. The wives — current and ex — of grass-roots Conservative party activists were among the most vociferous in approving the measure. They believe that a divorced non-earning woman who spent years raising children ought to receive a share of her husband's pension if their marriage fails.

But many feel that earmarking does not go far enough because the wife has to wait until her husband retires to get a share of his pension. In the meantime he might remarry, and should he then die, his widow and not his ex-wife would receive the remainder of his pension.

So the government is now working on a draft law that would allow pensions to be split at the time of divorce. This means that the wife would be able to get a slice of her husband's pension at the time they divorce.

The new measure is being delayed by the huge complexities involved in splitting company pensions —

MY EX-WIFE STILL INSISTS ON GETTING HALF OF EVERYTHING

-PILBROW-

especially final salary pension schemes, where there are defined benefits but no defined contributions.

Splitting also means that for the first time, a non-income earner — the divorcing housewife — would be allowed a pension in her own right. Until now, only taxpayers have been allowed to have a pension, its tax-free status a sort of quid pro quo for the years spent slaving away to keep the Inland Revenue's coffers full.

The problem with splitting pensions at the time a couple divorces is that the wife may get a fraction of her husband's pension: that is, she may get a much lower

transfer value than she might have got had she waited until her husband retired.

If marriages break up, they tend to do so at young-to-middle age. The husband has years of work ahead — and thus, years of building up a large retirement fund. So the wife may be settling for an artificially low share of her husband's final salary pension if she opts for splitting.

Of course, if she chooses to wait, she must depend on him keeping his job until retirement — by no means a certainty. But if she opts to take a split fund when her marriage fails, and then starts working — as many divorced women do — she could invest her share of her husband's fund in her new company scheme.

Pension splitting amounts to a break from centuries of pensions law and would usher in a unique product: a pension for non-income earners — such as housewives.

❓ What will happen to my pension if I retire early?

A It may lose a lot of its value. In fact, be prepared for a shock: you will lose a slice of your pension for every month you retire early. If you retire 10 years early, at 55, and have a final salary pension scheme, your fund will lose almost half its value. And those seeking to retire at 50 can expect to lose at least 70% of their pension fund.

The lesson for people aged 25 to 35 who want to retire early is to prepare now and not when you are over 45 when it will be too late. The reason is fairly simple: let's say you have done 40 years' service by the age 65, but you want to retire at 60. If you have a final salary scheme, which many employees do have, you will receive 1/60th of your final salary for every year worked. If you retire five years early, at 60, you would retire on 35/60ths instead of 40/60ths of your final salary a year. You would also lose a percentage of the value of your pension for each month spent in early retirement.

That works out at 30% off your pension if you leave five years (60 months) early,

making a total loss of about 40%. If you leave 10 years early you would lose 70% of your pension; 15 years early and you will have virtually no pension at all.

Money-purchase schemes and personal pensions are also ravaged by retiring early. Your money-purchase fund is used to buy an annuity, an annual income set according to your life expectancy and size of your pension fund. The problem is the longer you live, the smaller the annuity. So the earlier you retire, the worse your annuity rate. In other words, the younger you retire, the higher the price of every pound of annuity.

The only way you can offset such losses is to top up your fund now with your own additional voluntary contributions or invest in another retirement savings plan such as a Pep or the individual savings account, coming in 1999.

Today's thirtysomethings face a dark future if they fail to prepare now. By 2020, a quarter of all Europeans will be over the age of 65, estimates the Prudential.

At that age, every £1 of annual pension payment costs £10, so if you want to receive £10,000 a year, you will need a fund worth £100,000. Most people won't have that sum and face a difficult retirement. The reason is that people do not understand the cost of a pension. Experts advise everybody to take up any opportunity to join a company pension. Company money-purchase schemes typically contribute 5%-10% of your basic salary into your pension fund. This is like a bonus on your salary. Unless you plan to change jobs soon you ought to join the company scheme.

But you will have to contribute another 5% at least to produce a decent retirement fund — one that is equivalent to two-thirds of final salary.

Personal pensions do not generally benefit from the company's contribution unless your company undertakes to do so. In fact, many smaller companies now contribute to group personal pensions in which the entire staff may participate. If you retire early you will only receive the transfer value — the value built up at the point of departure — plus any bonus the company is prepared to make.

Certainly more employees are retiring early on good deals: companies sometimes offer generous retirement packages to encourage staff to retire early. But if you are self-employed your only safeguard against the costs of early retirement is to ensure your personal pension is fully topped up.

Q How do I check my pension performance?

A Once you have set up a pension, you may be tempted to sit back, relax, and think everything will be okay when you retire. However, since most pension funds are invested in the stockmarket, they rely on the fund manager's skills to make your money grow as much as possible. If they do a bad job, you could end up with a much smaller pension than you expected, so regularly checking its performance is essential.

The first point to remember is that if you have a final salary occupational pension scheme, then none of this matters. Your employer will make up your pension to its appropriate level whatever the fund's performance.

If you have a money purchase occupational scheme, or a personal pension, the money invested has to be used to buy an annuity on retirement, and in these cases the performance is crucial. Of course, the better the performance, the higher your retirement income.

But performance is not the only issue here: contribution levels are crucial. As one actuary has warned, money-purchase schemes may not always produce a decent retirement fund, often only 20% to 30% of final salaries, mainly due to low contributions averaging 8.2% of salary.

Money purchase occupational pensions provide annual statements showing the percentage growth in the fund, and the value of your particular contributions. However, most people have no idea whether this figure is good or bad.

There is no industry bench-mark for occupational pension funds so the best bet is to use the FT-SE 100 (Footsie) index as a yardstick. If the fund consistently underperforms the Footsie, then ask the pension fund's trustees for an

occupational scheme charges are so low.

The only exception is where the performance is really terrible – then higher charges could be outweighed by superior performance elsewhere.

For those with personal pensions, performance is a high priority, and is much easier to monitor. You can still use the Footsie as a yardstick but specialist publications such as Pensions Management magazine or your financial adviser will be able to tell you how your fund ranks in comparison with others on the market.

explanation. However, with your employer making contributions on your behalf, it will probably never make sense to leave the scheme on the basis of its performance. If you leave the company, the contributions will stop and it may then make sense to transfer your money into a personal pension if the performance is really bad. However, most advisers suggest leaving the money where it is because

The problem is, most personal pensions impose punitive charges if you leave the scheme early, so the decision as to whether to leave because of bad performance can be tricky.

Q What is the best way to top up my pension fund?

A This is a tricky area and you would be well advised to contact an expert pensions adviser. If in a company scheme, check with your pension department; if you have a personal pension, talk to your accountant or financial adviser.

A simple guide is that everyone should contribute as much to their pension fund as possible, or affordable.

Take company pension schemes first: your total contributions must not add up to more than 15% of your earnings (subject to a cash maximum of £13,140 in the 1998-99 tax year). For example, if you are paying 5% of your salary into the main company scheme, you could top it up with another 10% of your salary. Employers will also, of course, contribute a percentage.

The best way of topping up your company scheme is by making an additional voluntary contribution (AVC) – simply an extra contribution made by you if you feel you have enough money to do so. Many people approaching retirement make additional contributions to boost their final retirement fund. AVCs may be employer-run, or free-standing (that is, run by you).

Employer-run AVCs allow you to contribute up to the maximum limit to your company pension; any contributions attract tax relief up to your band, meaning that if you contribute 76p to the pension, the government will contribute 23p (based on 1996-97 tax rates). Your company pays for the administration of such schemes, so they are cheaper than free-standing AVCs.

However, with employer-run AVCs the investment choice is limited to the company's fund, none of the benefits may be taken as cash and you must stop contributions when you leave the company. Free-

standing AVCs are more flexible. A range of funds is available and you can use this scheme to contribute to a new company pension when you change jobs. But while free-standing AVCs give the same tax benefits, you have to pay their running costs, and none of the benefits can be taken as cash.

If you have a money purchase company pension instead of a final salary scheme, be sure that the maximum contributions are being invested to avoid underfunding. Personal pensions also apply strict limits on contributions, banded as a percentage of earnings depending on your age, from 17.5% aged 35 or less, up to 40% for those aged 61 or over.

So make sure you contribute the maximum allowable — or affordable. You can also supplement your pension by investing in savings schemes like Peps and Tessas. These have no up-front tax freedom, but any income or capital gains are tax-free, unlike pension funds, where you must pay tax on the annuity income.

If you are in the same tax band in employment as in retirement, then there is no meaningful difference between Peps and pensions; but if you drop down a band when you reach retirement, the pension looks appealing because you will be getting 40% up-front tax relief while paying 23% on the income.

Experts warn that many people working for smaller companies contribute little or nothing to a pension scheme — so be sure you're topped up.

● Taxation

INCOME TAX RATES	1998-99	97-98
20% on first	£4,300	£4,100
23% on next	£22,800	£22,000
40% on income over	£27,100	£26,100
Dividends for basic rate taxpayers	20%	20%
Interest etc for basic rate taxpayers	20%	20%
Certain trusts (eg, discretionary)	34%	34%

MAIN INCOME TAX RELIEFS	1998-99	97-98
Personal allowance (basic)	£4,195	£4,045
Personal allowance (age 65-74)	£5,410	£5,220
Personal allowance (age 75 & over)	£5,600	£5,400
Married couple's allowance (basic)*	£1,900	£1,830
Single parent families etc & maintenance*	£1,900	£1,830
Married couple's allowance (age 65-74)*	£3,305	£3,185
Married couple's allowance (age 75 & over)*	£3,345	£3,225
Income limit for age-related allowances	£16,200	£15,600
Blind person's allowance	£1,330	£1,280
Rent-a-room tax-free income	£4,250	£4,250
Mortgage interest relief-loans up to £30,000	10%	15%
Enterprise Investment Scheme at 20% **	£150,000	£100,000
Venture Capital Trust at 20% **	£150,000	£100,000

* allowances where relief is restricted to 15%

** also eligible for capital gains tax re-investment relief

PERSONAL PENSION CONTRIBUTIONS

Maximum contributions based on net relevant earnings

Age on 6 April	RAP* %	PPP %	98-99 £	97-98 £	Earnings Cap £	
35 or less	17.5	17.5	15,330	14,700	1998-99	87,600
36-45	17.5	20.0	17,520	16,800	1997-98	84,000
46-50	17.5	25.0	21,900	21,000	1996-97	82,200
51-55	20.0	30.0	26,280	25,200	1995-96	78,600
56-60	22.5	35.0	30,660	29,400	1994-95	76,800
61-74	27.5	40.0	35,040	33,600	1992-94	75,000
Life Ass	5.0	5.0	4,380	4,200	1991-92	71,400

* Retirement Annuity Plans (started pre 1.7.88): no cap

BASIC STATE PENSION 1998-99 1997-98

	1998-99	1997-98
Single person per year	£3,364.40	£3,247.40
Dependant's addition per year	£2,012.40	£1,942.20
Married couple total per year	£5,376.80	£5,189.60

EMPLOYEE BENEFITS	1998-99	1997-98
Profit sharing scheme: 10% of earnings max	£8,000	£8,000
Savings-related share options per month	£250	£250
Approved Share Option Plans	£30,000	£30,000
Cheap loan benefit tax-free if loan is up to	£5,000	£5,000
Golden handshake exemption	£30,000	£30,000
Mobile telephone assessment	£200	£200
Relocation expenses max tax-free	£8,000	£8,000
Profit related pay tax-free: 20% of pay max	£2,000*	£4,000**

* for profit periods starting 1999 ceiling reduced to £1,000

** for profit periods starting 1998 ceiling reduced to £2,000

CAR BENEFIT 1997-99

Business use pa up to	2,500 miles	2,500-17,999 & 2nd cars	18,000 miles & over
% list price	35%	$23^1/_3$%	$11^2/_3$%
Max chargeable	£28,000	£18,666.67	£9,333.33

- List price includes cost of optional extras
- Cars aged at least 4 years on 5 April: 1/3 off scale rate
- 2nd cars with 18,000 business miles or more: 1/3 off scale rate
- Cars aged 15 years or more on 5 April & with value of £15,000 or more: taxed at current market value
- Private use of van: under 4 yrs £500; 4 yrs & over £350

CAR FUEL

CAR FUEL		1,400cc or less	1,401–2,000cc	Over 2,000cc
1998-99	Petrol	£1,010	£1,280	£1,890
	Diesel	£1,280	£1,280	£1,890
1997-98	Petrol	£800	£1,010	£1,490
	Diesel	£740	£740	£940

New mileage allowances for employee cars
The rate of mileage allowance that employees can claim when using their own car for business travel during 1997/98 are given below. Self-employed people with a turnover that is not more than the current VAT registration limit of £48,000 may also be able to use these rates rather than making separate claims for petrol, servicing, capital allowances on the car etc.

Tax-free rate per mile

Size of car engine	On the first 4,000 miles in the tax year		On each mile over 4,000 miles in the tax year	
	1996-97	1997-98	1996-97	1997-98
Up to 1,000cc	27p	28p	16p	17p
1,000–1,500cc	34p	35p	19p	20p
1,501–2,000cc	43p	45p	23p	25p
over 2,000cc	61p	63p	33p	36p

STAMP DUTY

Land: 1% on total value if over £60,000
Stocks and marketable securities 1/2%

NATIONAL INSURANCE CONTRIBUTIONS

Class 1 Employees (rates calculated on total earnings)

1998-99 contracted into SERPS		1997-98 contracted into SERPS	
Earnings pw	Employee	Earnings pw	Employee
Below £64	NIL	Below £62	NIL
£64-£485	2% of £64 plus 10% of excess	£62-£465	2% of £62 plus 10% of excess
Over £485	£43.38pw	Over £465	£41.54pw
Earnings pw	Employer	Earnings pw	Employer
Below £64	NIL	Below £62	NIL
£64-£109.99	3%	£62-£109.99	3%
£110-£154.99	5%	£110-£154.99	5%
£155-£209.99	7%	£155-£209.99	7%
£210 & over	10%	£210 & over	10%

Certain married women: reduced employee rate 3.85%

Contracted out of SERPS – final salary schemes	1998-99	1997-98
Reduction on band earnings	£64-£485	£62-£465
Employer rate reduction	3%	3%
Employee rate reduction	1.6%	1.6%

Contracted out rebate on personal pensions 1997-99

Age at end of prior tax year:	20	21	22	23	24	25	26	27	28	29	30	31	32	33
Rebate* % of band earnings:	3.6	3.7	3.7	3.8	3.8	3.9	3.9	4.0	4.0	4.1	4.2	4.2	4.3	4.3

Age at end of prior tax year:	34	35	36	37	38	39	40	41	42	43	44	45	46+
Rebate* % of band earnings:	4.4	4.5	4.7	4.9	5.0	5.2	5.4	5.6	6.0	6.7	7.4	8.2	9.0

* Plus tax relief on employee contribution: 0.48%

NATIONAL INSURANCE CONTRIBUTIONS

continued from previous page
Earnings limits

	1998-99			1997-98		
	Weekly	Monthly	Annual	Weekly	Monthly	Annual
Lower	£64	£277	£3,328	£62	£269	£3,224
Upper	£485	£2,102	£25,220	£465	£2,015	£24,180

Class 1A: on value of car benefit & car fuel: 10%

Self-employed	1998-99	1997-98
Class 2 Flat rate	£6.35pw £330.20pa	£6.15pw £319.80pa
if earnings over	£3,590pa	£3,480pa
Class 4 Rate	6% (max £1,074.60)	6% (max £1,030.20)
on profits	£7,310-£25,220pa	£7,010-£24,180pa
Voluntary		
Class 3 Flat rate	£6.25pw £325.00pa	£6.05pw £314.60pa

INHERITANCE TAX RATES

	1998-99	1997-98
Nil-rate band	£223,000	£215,000
Rate of tax on excess	40%	40%
Transfers to and from certain trusts	20%	20%
Overseas domiciled spouse exemption	£55,000	£55,000
Business Property and Agricultural Reliefs		
Owner-occupied and farm tenancies	100%	100%
Let farmland	100%	100%
Unincorporated businesses	100%	100%
Unquoted and AIM/USM companies	100%	100%
Certain other business assets	50%	50%

Reduced tax charge on gifts within 7 years of death

Years before death:	0-3	3-4	4-5	5-6	6-7
% of death charge:	100%	80%	60%	40%	20%

Annual exempt gifts: £3,000 per donor, £250 per donee

CAPITAL GAINS TAX RATES

	1998–99	1997–98
Individuals as income tax rates		
Certain trusts (eg, discretionary)	34%	34%
Annual Exemptions		
Individuals, personal representatives, etc	£6,800	£6,500
Trusts generally	£3,400	£3,250
Chattels (5/3 taxable on excess)	£6,000	£6,000

Retirement Relief from age 50 or earlier ill-health

Exemption: 100% of gain up to £250,000; 50% on next £750,000

PERSONAL EQUITY PLAN (PEP) 1997-99

General PEP & EU unit and investment trust limit	£6,000
Non-EU unit and investment trust limit	£1,500
Plus single company limit	£3,000

CORPORATION TAX

	to 31.3.99	to 31.3.98
Full Rate	31%	31%
Small Companies Rate	21%	21%
Small Companies Limit	£300,000	£300,000
Effective Marginal Rate	33.5%	33.5%
Upper Marginal Limit	£1,500,000	£1,500,000
	1998–99	1997–98
Advance Corporation Tax on dividend plus ACT	20%	20%

MAIN CAPITAL ALLOWANCES

Plant and Machinery, Patent Rights,
Know-How: *25% pa
Certain long-life Plant and Machinery
bought after 25.11.96:   *6% pa
Motor Cars: *25% pa
                                      max £3,000 pa

*Writing down allowance (reducing balance)

Enterprise Zone Buildings: initial allowance 100%
Scientific Research: initial allowance 100%
Industrial and Agricultural Buildings, Hotels, Docks, etc:
Writing down allowance (straight line)   4% pa

VALUE ADDED TAX Standard Rate: 17.5%

Domestic fuel and power: 8%
Registration level: to 31.3.98 £49,000, from 1.4.98 £50,000

Cash scheme turnover limit: £350,000
Car fuel: Vatable outputs based on car fuel benefit charge

MAIN DUE DATES FOR TAX PAYMENT

Income Tax and Capital Gains Tax – Self-Assessment
31 Jan in tax year: pay 50% based upon previous year's income
tax charge, less tax deducted at source
Following 31 July: pay balance of estimated tax
Following 31 Jan: make final settlement of income tax
and all CGT

Inheritance Tax
Death: normally 6 months after month of death
Lifetime transfer 6 April-30 Sept; 30 April in following year
Lifetime transfer 1 Oct-5 April; 6 months after
month of transfer

Corporation Tax
Pay & File – 9 months after accounting period

All charts courtesy of Taxbriefs Specialist Financial Publishers,
2-5 Benjamin Street, London EC1M 5QL. Tel: 0171-250 0967

Useful telephone numbers

TRADE & REGULATORY BODIES

Financial Services Authority
(overall regulator)
Gavrelle House
2-14 Bunhill Row
London EC17 8RA
TEL: 0171-638 1240

Investment Management
Regulatory Organisation
(regulates fund managers,
unit trusts, portfolio
managers)
Lloyds Chambers
1 Portsoken Street
London E1 8BT
TEL: 0171-390 5000

Personal Investment
Authority (regulates
financial advisers)
1 Canada Square
7th Floor
Canary Wharf
London E14 5AZ
TEL: 0171-538 8860

Securities & Futures
Authority (regulates the
stockmarket, foreign
exchange, futures and
options markets)
Cottons Centre
Cottons Lane
London SE1 2QB
TEL: 0171-378 9000

Association of British
Insurers (insurers'
professional body)
51 Gresham Street
London EC2V 7HQ
TEL: 0171-600 3333

Independent Financial
Advisers' Promotion
(for a list of financial
advisers and insurance
brokers in your area). Central
number: 0117-971 1177

British Insurance & Investment
Brokers' Association (BIIBA).
14, Bevis Marks,
London EC3A 7NT.
0171-623 9043

OMBUDSMEN (to lodge personal complaints)

Banking Ombudsman
70 Gray's Inn Road
London WC1X 8NB
TEL: 0171-404 9944

Pensions Ombudsman
11 Belgrave Road
London SW1V 1RB
TEL: 0171-834 9144

Insurance Ombudsman
City Gate One
135 Park Street
London SE1 9EA
TEL: 0171-928 4488

The Adjudicator (Inland Revenue and VAT ombudsman)
3rd Floor, Haymarket House
28 Haymarket,
London SW1Y 4SP
TEL: 0171-930 2292

Building Societies Ombudsman
Millbank Tower
Millbank Road
London SW1P 4XS
TEL: 0171-931 0044

The Building Societies Association
3 Savile Row
London W1X 1AF
TEL: 0171-437 0655

(The Council of Mortgage Lenders is based at same address & telephone)

National Consumer Council
20 Grosvenor Gardens
London SW1W 0DH
TEL: 0171-730 3469

Consumers Association
2 Marylebone Road
London NW1 4DF
TEL: 0171-830 6000

National Association of Estate Agents
Arbon House
21 Jury Street
Warwick CV34 4EH
TEL: 01926-496 800

Notes

Notes

Notes

Notes

Notes

Notes

Also available

● Guide to Your Home:

How To Buy, Sell and Pay for It by Diana Wright

Are you thinking of buying a home?

- Should you choose a fixed or variable rate mortgage?
- How can you save money on insurance?
- How do you get the best out of an estate agent?
- What is the best mortgage for a second-time buyer?

0 00 653066 4   **HarperColllins Paperbacks**   **£7.99**

● Guide to Your Retirement:

How To Plan Wisely for Later Life by Diana Wright

Are you approaching retirement? Do you know:

- How much your pension will be?
- How to trace pensions from previous employers?
- Whether you should take the lump sum from your pension scheme?
- What sort of annuity should you buy and what difference a good choice would make?
- Where to find good financial advice?
- What sort of insurance you need?

0 00 638707 1   **HarperColllins Paperbacks**   **£6.99**

Guide to Tax-free Savings:

How to Make Your Money
Work Hardest For You by Christopher Gilchrist

Are you making the most of your savings and investments?

- how moving your savings into tax-free schemes can boost your returns
- how to work out what you need to save for retirement and the best tax-exempt ways to do so
- the differences between lower-risk, moderate-risk and high-risk schemes and how much each could produce for you
- identifying the saving and investment plans that offer the best value for money
- the best plans for short-term and longer-term savings

0 00 638703 9   HarperColllins Paperbacks   £6.99

THE SUNDAY TIMES
BOOKSHOP

To order any of The Sunday Times Personal Finance Guides featured in the back of this book or additional copies of this book at prices reduced from the suggested retail price please call or complete and post the coupon below

● You can also buy ANY English-language book currently in print

● FREE UK p&p ● Delivery in 7-10 days, subject to availability

● 24-hour telephone ordering service. Staff available 9am to 4pm Saturday, 10am to 4pm Sunday and 8am to 6pm, Monday through Friday

TO ORDER CALL: 0990 134 459

Call +44 990 134 459 from overseas and the Republic of Ireland, fax +44 1326 374 888. e-mail: bookshop@sunday-times.co.uk

Or post this coupon to: News Books, PO Box 345, Falmouth, TR11 2YX
Please send me these books (order additional titles on a separate sheet):

Qty	Title/Author	Total
	The Sunday Times Guide to Your Home RRP £7.99 now £6.99	
	The Sunday Times Guide to Your Retirement RRP £6.99 now £5.99	
	The Sunday Times Guide to Tax-Free Savings RRP £6.99 now £5.99	
	The Sunday Times 50 Essential Questions on Money RRP £6.99 now £5.99	

Surname .... Initial .... Title ....

Address ....

....

Postcode .... Tel ....

I enclose cheque/PO(s) payable to NEWS BOOKS for a total of £ ....

Please write your name and address on the back of all cheques. *For Republic of Ireland and overseas orders add 20% to total book cost. Delivery by airmail in Europe, surface to rest of world. (Airmail outside Europe add 35%.) The RRP of a book can be subject to change by publisher without prior notice.* Tick box if you prefer not to receive details of other offers ☐

Or debit my Mastercard/Visa/AmEx, Switch or Delta account no:

50

Print Name .... Expiry Date ....

Signature .... Date ....